To my sweet Nar,
So awesome meeting you!
Hope you enjoy the book!
Share it with your girls!
Keep being the awesome person
you are!
Keep doing the important SEL
work!
And, most importantly, Keep
ROCKIN' your own world!

♡ Sheira

P.S. Hugs & kisses to Dave !!!

Motiv8

8 Ways To ROCK
Your Own World

Sheira Brayer

ISBN 978-0-692-901892

Design by Cory Rosenberg

Edited by Ayden Skye

Printed in the United States of America

First paperback edition

The advice contained within this book does not constitute, or serve as a substitute for, professional psychological treatment, therapy, or other types of professional advice or intervention.

To contact the author, visit **www.sheirabrayer.com**.

DEDICATION

To my mother for giving me life.

To my daughter for giving it meaning.

CONTENTS

MUSIC

B ecause I believe in the power of music, each chapter[1] features an original companion song written by yours truly to reinforce the concepts presented. All songs listed below plus 3 bonus tracks are available online including on iTunes and Spotify for your listening pleasure.

MEDITATION..............*Breathe*

OPTIMISM......................*Change Your Mind*

TOLERANCE.................*We're All The Same*

INTUITION.....................*A Way Will Be Shown*

VIBE..................................*Givin' It Out Again*

ATTITUDE......................*It's Not What You Say It's How You Say It*

THANKFULNESS.........*Thank U*

EXPRESSION................*Gift of Song*

Bonus tracks:

A Song for Ayden – written for my daughter

Don't Have Your Eyes – written by my daughter

A Mother's Love – written for my grandmother

---

[1] Except "Thankfulness."

DISCLAIMER

This book is meant for both moms and their teen daughters. When I decided to write this, my very first thought was, "Alright, let's get real. Teenage girls aren't going to want to read this if their *mothers* are reading it. In fact, they'll run in the opposite direction!" But then I thought about it again... and I quickly realized that, even if today's girls might not *want* to at first, they *should* be reading the same book as their mothers. Let me guess, gals: you totally disagree. I thought you might. So I came prepared — here are the top three reasons why this book makes more sense than you might think:

Reason #1: As much as teenage girls are convinced that their mothers can sometimes be their nemesis, their worst nightmare, or the devil incarnate, the truth is that girls want to be connected to their moms. Likewise, no matter how frustrating or immature their daughters can be, mothers want to be there for their daughters every step of the way. So basically, no matter how you slice it, a strong mother-daughter bond is a non-negotiable part of life — and the only way to strengthen that bond is to have both parties at the same table.

Reason #2: Every woman was once a girl, and every girl will eventually become a woman. Don't just read this for Present You — read it for Past You, and Future You too! When women remember where they came from, and girls gain insight into where they're headed, everyone benefits. We share so many of the same concerns, aspirations, insecurities, and emotions. And — on the flip side — it's about time we start appreciating (as opposed to disparaging) our differences.

And finally, **Reason #3:** It's my book and I'll do what I want!

Let me ask you a question: Are you happy that you're female? I'm sure few people, if any, have asked you this question before. But really think about it for a second. Are you relieved to be able to let out your emotions without the fear of being called a wuss? Are you excited to be able to experience the miracle of giving birth? Are you proud to be part of a long lineage of incredible women who have helped shape the world?

Undoubtedly, there will be some days when your answer to that question will be a resounding "HELL NO!" Days when you feel like no one understands you. Days when you're doubled over in pain from cramps. Days when it hits you hard that women still only make $0.78 for every $1 that a man makes. But the fact of the matter is days like those are the reason we need to start believing in the power of the female.

Society is still articulated in a predominantly male voice. It's mostly men who make laws. It's mostly men who run companies. It's mostly men who are acknowledged for big accomplishments. I don't bring up this fact for the sake of bashing men, but rather to shed light on the startling *lack of balance* in today's society. The word "equality" is the one that gets the most airtime in discussions of women's rights — and understandably so — but I believe the true goal is bal-ance. Balance, by definition, is the even distribution of elements to ensure that the larger entity doesn't fall apart. The simple fact is, all variations of gender, race, religion, sexuality, and creed are needed to create this balance.

The good news is we are making incredible strides! In the last 95 years, we've made more advancements than in all the thousands of years preceding it combined. Just fifty years ago, only 6% of doctors, 3% of lawyers, and fewer than 1% of engineers were women. Back then, women weren't allowed to compete in the Boston Marathon, and — here's a good one — women needed their husband's permis-sion to get a credit card. What's more, this past decade has proved that it's not just about fundamental rights like voting and owning money — now it's about empowering women and girls to be every-thing they want to be. From viral video campaigns like Dove's and Pantene's, to movies like *Girl Rising* and *Brave,* to movements such as Women For Women International, Equality Now, and Chime For Change… it's happening. Girl power isn't just a cute saying any-more — it's a real thing.

We've made so much progress and should be so proud, but we can't let up now. We still have so far to go to reach that pivotal point of balance. If we get complacent, we'll never get there. We must contin-ue forging ahead, plowing through obstacles, and showing our peers — and ourselves — what we're capable of.

It's easy to blame men for our hindered influence in modern society. But when we delve into the heart of the issue, it becomes evident that it may not just be men who are stopping us from becoming all that we can be; it may be ourselves. In conversing with women and girls from all walks of life, I see an inordinate amount of pettiness, jealousy, insecurity, and downright meanness. The movie *Mean Girls* tackles this concept head-on, and we would all do ourselves a big favor to learn from it. The IndieFlix documentary *Finding Kind* provides another, real-life example of this undeniable negativity. In it, the film's creators — Lauren Parsekian and Molly Thompson — travel the country from coast to coast interviewing women and girls about their experiences. One of the most salient moments was when they interviewed grown women who recalled being tormented, put down, and ridiculed in their tween/teen years. To this day, they break down and weep as they recount how badly it made them feel. We need to remember that experiences are cumulative. Some believe that negative school experiences are transient, but they are anything but. Females are capable of being vicious when they feel wronged. Honoring our contribution to the current imbalance in society means putting an end to the emotional hurt that often defines our formative years. As the first female Secretary of State Madeline Albright so clearly put it: "There is a special place in hell for women who don't help other women." If we want to be empowered, we must start by empowering each other.

The mother-daughter relationship is the starting point for that transformation.

Moms, we are raising the women who will further — and hopefully conquer — our cause. This could be the generation that changes everything. This could be the generation that finally sees the election of a female President. This could be the generation that closes the wage gap. This could be the generation... but only if all of its members are instilled with confidence, respect, determination, and a strong sense of self. We need to show our daughters how to leverage their many strengths, and we must take this role very seriously. If your own challenging upbringing is hindering your ability to help your daughter, then you must seek guidance in some form. If we're not being all that we want our daughters to be, or at least growing and learning alongside them, then we're not fulfilling our role as a parent.

Now, I'm not saying it's easy to parent a tween/teen girl. Good ol' Mother Nature (emphasis on "Mother"!) truly has a way of giving you a run for your money. One minute, your daughter is asking for a favor; the next, she's telling you to get lost. The volatile nature of young girls can be exhausting, no question. But if you can remember what *you* were like as a teenager, you can start to understand that it's not necessarily toward *you* that the occasional (or not so occasional) rage is directed. Also, when you learn to see how your own behavior affects the relationship, you'll be one step closer to not only raising a happier daughter, but also maintaining a healthier connection with her.

As for all the teen girls out there, I have to give you a lot of credit — being a teen girl today is *way* harder than when I was growing up. Back in the day, there were only a few ways to feel embarrassed or be ridiculed in front of others. Today, there are hundreds — and it's not just in front of your friends, but potentially in front of the whole world — and in HD! The amount of scrutiny and pressure you experience simply boggles the mind — and the hardest part for me is seeing how much pressure you put *yourselves* under. The pressure to be, look, talk and behave perfectly can really add up. I know, I've been there. I'm imagining you sometimes think to yourself "there must be a better way." Well, I'm here to tell you there *is*.

Feeling good in your own skin takes time.
Keep your heart and mind open,
and be patient.

My goal is to open you up to how fabulous you are. This book is what I refer to as a "toolbox." It covers 8 essential tools that will help teen girls and their moms build confidence, manage stress, and feel good in their own skin. Girls, if you can learn these things while you're young, you'll be much better off down the road. And, moms, it's never too late to learn new things — especially alongside your daughter(s)!

My wish for any woman or girl reading this, no matter what your situation, is that the skills I outline trigger an "a-ha" moment — that lead you to realize how to help yourself in ways you never could before. I hope that Motiv8 lives up to its name, and motivates you to make change — in your life, in relationships, social circles, and ultimately, your communities.

But before we can get there, we have to start at the core. We have to start with just one amazing, valuable, irreplaceable person. We have to start with you.

INTRODUCTION

I 've always been fascinated with the concept of "motivation." Some of us seem to be truly self-motivated, while others seem to be sloths on the couch of life. What is that about? Some of it can be attributed to heredity, but that's only a small part of it. I came across something else — something far more telling — about human beings.

Some people believe that motivation is the first step to accomplishing a goal. As it turns out, the people who are the most motivated are the ones who realize that isn't true.

MOTIVATION EXPLAINED

We are always trying to accomplish a thousand things at once. Clean out the attic. Learn French. Eat healthy. Marry Adam Levine in a picturesque ceremony on the beach in Aruba. But often, especially when it's a challenge (Adam Levine is already taken), we wait and wait and never take that first step. We then conclude, "well, I guess I'm just not motivated," as if motivation is a little fairy with a pink tutu and a magic wand that sprinkles motivational pixie dust on your lazy self and then flies off into the abyss.

According to John Maxwell's book *Failing Forward: Turning Mistakes into Stepping Stones for Success,* motivation is actually never the first step in making things happen. Let me repeat that: *motivation is never the first step in making things happen.* The first step is *making a decision.* Anything that requires hard work starts with a firm and unwavering decision that it will be so.

The next and probably most important step is Nike's tagline: JUST DO IT. The power in taking action, no matter how insignificant it may seem, cannot be overstated. For example, if you want to get more physically fit, the simple act of putting on your sneakers is critical. Granted, it also might be a good idea to take a few steps with your sneakers on. But for some of us, just putting on our sneakers is half the battle. Once you begin to take action consistently, you start to see results. And it's those results that give you the motivation you need to keep going and reach your goal!

It's usually the smallest of actions that can cause the cogs of momentum to move in our favor.

Take me, for example. I have wanted to write a book for years now, and it was literally the day that I wrote just one sentence in a Word document that got the ball rolling! I remember watching the cursor move as I typed and saying to myself, "I'm doing it! I'm actually doing it!"

MY BIG TOMAHAWK MOMENT

Back in 2000, I was on a JetBlue flight from Florida to New York with my twin sister reading a book she'd recommended called *You'll See It When You Believe It* by Dr. Wayne Dyer. As I was reading it, I remember saying in my head "Oh boy, my mother could really use this; she can be so negative," and "Ugh, my husband does that all the time; if he just read this, he would be transformed!" Then, I distinctly remember my sister tapping me on the shoulder, and without any hesitation, asked, "Are you reading this book with other people in mind?" I was too embarrassed to admit it, so I said, "No." She looked at me as only she can, with her chin down, eyebrows at full tilt and said, "Really?" No. Not really. And she knew it.

The next morning, on May 3, 2000 (it was such a monumental event in my life that I never forgot the date), I was sitting at my kitchen table, still in a total tizzy over this book. I felt confused, annoyed, and overwhelmed by all the information I had read. Just as I was trying to make sense of it all, I suddenly felt this visceral, physical shift and a weight the size of a boulder evaporating off of my shoulders. I know this sounds a little nuts, but I could have sworn I heard a little voice in my head say, "It's all about you, Sheira. It's all about you." Kind of creepy, but fascinating nonetheless. I sat there at my kitchen table in stunned silence. It was the most powerful "a ha," light-bulb, OMG, Satori[2] moment I had ever experienced.

All of those emotions I had about my mother, my husband, and everyone else in my life were simply distractions. They were a way to shift the focus of responsibility from myself to another target. It was my ego talking: "I'm not the one with the problem, they are!" And I truly believed that for a *long, long* time. But the little voice in my head was right! It's all about me. I have the power to change anything I want *by changing myself.*

---

[2] Satori is Japanese for sudden awakening or looking into one's own nature.

It's so easy to blame everything and
everyone outside of us for the problems
in our lives, but that only results in
frustration — never in change.

My hope for you is that reading these words begins to draw your focus inward toward your own awareness, emotions, strengths, and shortcomings. If you can consciously do that, minute by minute, day by day, you can literally change your life. I call it *"living from inside-out."* As a society, we spend so much time focusing on our relationships with everyone around us (parents, siblings, teachers, kids, neighbors, co-workers, etc.) that we begin to miss out on cultivating the most important relationship of them all — the one we have with ourselves! Just like a camera's focus can be adjusted to put the background image in or out of focus, you too can shift the focus from all those background distractions (gossip, news, drama, cell phones, iPads, siblings, girlfriends, boyfriends, etc.) to focus on *you*, the most important subject of your life's story.

Using the word MOTIVATE as an acronym, the chapters that follow will take you through eight critical skills that are intended to open you to new ideas which, in turn, will help you reduce your stress level, increase your awareness and feel more in control of your life.

MEDITATION

To clear out my mind

When I say the word "meditation," what is the first image that is conjured up in your mind? Is it a swami dude, sitting on the ground with legs crossed at the knees while chanting (like this?)

If that's the visual you have, you're not alone. It's commonly misconstrued that meditation is a religious practice (probably because it has its origins there). Today, the practice of meditation is widely recommended and scientifically proven to be one of the most highly effective stress reduction techniques. The textbook definition of the word *meditate* is "to engage in mental exercise (as concentration on one's breathing or repetition of a word or sound, known as a mantra) for the purpose of reaching a heightened level of awareness." So, in essence, meditation allows you to gain control over your mind, instead of your mind controlling you. On the whole, we girls and women tend to do the latter — we think, ponder, worry, obsess, analyze, over-analyze... then we lather, rinse, and repeat. And we wonder why there's so much drama in our lives!

Here's a question: When you wake up in the morning, after getting out of bed and before leaving the house… what do you do? Yes, you brush your teeth. Yes, you get dressed. Yes, you then decide you don't like what you're wearing, take that off, and get dressed again. But there's something else that you do that's more important than you might think: you go to the bathroom. Ever think about why you do that? Simple. If you didn't, your body would build up with toxins and you would get really sick. And maybe even die. And that would suck.

To coin a new SAT analogy, meditation is to the mind what pooping is to your body. Negative thoughts are toxic to the mind. Women and girls are especially burdened by a never-ending build-up of toxic thoughts. "I'm not pretty enough." "My thighs are too fat." "Everyone else has their lives figured out and I'm a hot mess!" Everything in your life starts with a thought. Those thoughts lead to beliefs, which lead to words, which lead to actions. The danger lies not in the thought itself, but in the *belief* of the thought; this is why we must go straight to the source. If we don't take the time each day to flush out toxic thoughts, we're hurting ourselves more than we realize. Luckily, meditation is a very accessible way to reverse the damage.

THE PRACTICE OF MEDITATION

Now, I know what you're probably thinking; I thought it too when I first gave meditation a shot: "Is this a joke? Not think? Me? Yeah, right." If your mind is anything like mine before I started meditating (and if it is, G-d bless you), it's comparable to a hamster wheel going 'round and 'round in perpetual motion. But hey folks, it's called the *practice* of meditation for a reason — it takes a lot of practice! To refer back to our renewed concept of motivation, once I made the *decision* to meditate consistently, I became more skilled over time, and that made me curious as to how far I could actually go. Today, I can say with unequivocal certainty that meditation has transformed my life. If

I had known about this when I was younger, I'm pretty sure it would have helped me be less of a bitch to my mother. Sorry Mom!

So now the question becomes, how do we incorporate meditation into our daily lives? Well, consider the amount of things we make time for that have absolutely zero impact on our quality of life. We do certain things routinely — wash our hands, watch TV, check our cell phones, use social media — without even blinking. And yet, spending a few minutes every day quieting our minds, focusing on our breath, and being more present is considered a big pain-in-the-butt chore! If you can make time for a bevy of mindless activities, you can certainly make time for something that can profoundly change the quality of your life.

If you don't go within, you'll go without.

MEDITATION EACH DAY KEEPS THE DOCTOR AWAY

Think of meditation as a prevention technique. People who want to avoid heart attacks take an aspirin every day. People who want to avoid osteoporosis lift weights. So, logically, people who want to avoid anxiety, impatience, mental clutter, and premature aging should practice meditation. I'm pretty sure that would include 99.9999% of humanoids.

If the prevention benefits mentioned above are not enough to convince you about the miracle of meditation, you should also know that, in addition to reducing stress and anxiety, meditation can:

- Lower your blood pressure (a key indicator of good health)

- Boost your natural immune system against all kinds of diseases

- Act as an anti-inflammatory — which is awesome considering inflammation in the body is a precursor to all kinds of physical ailments including skin issues (yes, girls, meditation can help with pimples!)

- Increase creativity.

Those are just a few of the benefits of meditation. And, the best part of all? No side effects!

LET'S DO THIS

The best time to meditate is at the beginning of your day. It's a great way to set your intentions and start your day off on the right foot. Taking a few minutes to focus solely on yourself — which, as moms, we know can often fall by the wayside — is an excellent example to set for our daughters. And, as an added bonus for both parties, it's the ultimate stress reducer for the times when your mother/daughter is getting on your nerves. If that's not an incentive, I don't know what is! Think of it as a time-released capsule that provides you with extra patience, understanding, and clarity throughout your day. It's 100% free and doctor recommended!

If you're just beginning, try meditating for just five minutes in the morning, every day. Insert it as a regular daily activity, perhaps after showering and brushing your teeth. Making it a ritual will ensure that it's not viewed as optional. As you continue practicing, you can increase the duration from five minutes to ten, fifteen, or twenty. Twenty minutes, twice a day, is ideal. Don't let this number scare you; it's something you can work toward. If you can't do twenty minutes, just do what you can.

Just like there's no one right way to
exercise or study, there's no one right way
to meditate.

Meditation reveals an interesting dichotomy: on one hand, it follows a particular set of guidelines, and on the other hand, it's totally customizable. Some prefer to meditate sitting upright on a chair; others (like myself) prefer to meditate lying on their backs. Some prefer to meditate guided by a soothing voice, music, or ambient sounds, like running water or white noise; others (like myself) prefer to meditate in silence. But that's the beauty of meditation — there's no one right way to do it. All forms can be effective, depending on the willingness of the practitioner. Try a few different methods and find the one that suits you best.

Meditation is all about breath. Focusing on the breath is what allows us to get out of our own heads, even if just for a few seconds. One of the best ways to get into a solid breathing rhythm is to use imagery. For example, imagine a bowl of soup in front of you. When you inhale, you're smelling the soup, and when you exhale, you're blowing on the soup. Another thing you can notice is that when you exhale from your nose, the air is warm, and when you inhale, it's cooler. So to take the focus away from your mind and the thoughts that often dictate its activity, feel that sensation, and repeat the phrase "in, cold... out, warm" in your mind.

A third technique that never fails to propel me into a semi-hypnotic state is called "The Third Eye." With your eyes closed, take a few deep breaths and then very slowly cross your eyes so that they land on the bridge of your nose, where an imaginary "third eye" would be.

With each long exhale, feel yourself falling deeper and deeper into an abyss of peace.

MINI MEDITATION SESSIONS

Although it's ideal to set time aside, meditation does not always have to be scheduled. Meditation "mini sessions," as I like to call them, are an incredibly helpful way to counteract stressful situations on an as-needed basis. For example, girls, let's say you're dealing with friend drama at school. As you know, drama can escalate in minutes to seemingly outrageous proportions. If you feel yourself starting to get sucked in like a dust bunny into a vacuum cleaner, that's your cue to take a minute or two to do some deep breathing. Afterwards you'll be in a much better state to make a decision that will serve you best. You might more consciously decide to keep going, replying, posting, or spewing. Or, dare I say, you might choose to step out of the conversation. Meditation has the power to help you acknowledge the merit of a different route — a route that *you* choose and *you* control. Simply deciding that you're not going to be a part of the negativity can give you an incredible sense of empowerment. You only need to do it once to feel the euphoria. Try it if you don't believe me!

Not taking any action is an action unto itself.
And sometimes it's the best action to take.

Moms, here's an opportunity for you. The next time you're stuck in traffic and you realize you're going to be late to a meeting or to pick up your child, or to wherever you're going, look at it as a chance for you to take a deep breath, and re-process the situation. As you're in the car, staring at the sea of vehicles surrounding you, take a second and say to yourself: "I'm going to smell the soup and blow on the soup five times right now." You can't make those cars disappear; (only Jim Carrey in *Bruce Almighty* can do that). So given the reality of the traffic, focusing on your breathing is your best bet. It's also another awesome way to model behavior for your daughter. Traffic, like everything else you have no control over, is one of those phenomena that can either enrage you or make you more mindful. Which do you choose?

The ultimate multipurpose de-stressing tool, meditation can also help alleviate the burden of a stressful (or seemingly stressful) situation *after* it happens. Whether it's fighting with a family member, reviewing your never-ending to-do list, or dropping a gallon of milk down your basement stairs while bringing in the groceries (although I wouldn't know, because that exact situation definitely did not happen to me), there's always a way to backtrack after the fact. Meditation can easily help reverse the damage of losing it with your kids, lamenting the shortage of hours in a day, and/or watching milk spill all over your basement floor as you look on in horror. [Insert "there's no use crying over spilled milk" joke here.]

NOT SO FAST....

There's another interesting technique that works in conjunction with meditation that has a similar calming effect: slowing down your speech. When I was a teenager, I did everything quickly: walking, thinking, eating, and, of course, talking. When I would talk to my mother in "Teen" (its own language in which every other word is "like"), she would look at me and say, in her Israeli accent, "Eh, Sheira, stop talking so fast. You're going to get a speeding ticket." She was right, but the reason why only dawned on me later in life. By speaking too quickly, we don't allow ourselves the opportunity to think about what's coming out of our mouths. When we're intentional and selective with our words, we're much more in control.

You...decide...how...quickly...or...slowly...
you...want...to...speak.

We've all said things that we've immediately regretted. Had we taken even just a nanosecond of a pause before we said it, we'd likely have been better off. So if you want to avoid getting a "speeding ticket" (and believe me the fine can be pretty steep), try putting on the brakes when it comes to the pace of your speech. This also goes for text or e-mail communication. It's so easy to angrily punch some letters and press "Send" — but just like spoken words, you can't take them back 30 seconds later when you regret saying them. *Think* before you speak (or type).

SELF-INQUIRY

A final thought on the practice of meditation: It's not only a way to feel calmer; it's also a way to get to the root of our mind's most pressing conflicts. It's pretty logical when you think about it. When our mind is quiet we have an open forum to ask ourselves questions. For example, if you find yourself constantly feeling overwhelmed at having too much to do — which I believe holds true for many girls and women — you may want to ask yourself, as you're quieting your mind: "Why do I constantly feel overwhelmed? What can I do to feel more balanced?" Don't try to come up with answers right away; don't try to immediately fix it. Just sit with the emotion of feeling overwhelmed. At some point, as if by magic, the answer will begin to surface.

When I first started to meditate, I asked myself the aforementioned question. And for a few sessions, when I still wasn't very good at quieting my mind, I would ask it, get nothing, and then immediately be tempted to quit meditating and go about my business. But a few weeks into it, once I started getting better at going deeper within and tuning out the world, an answer seemed to hit me out of nowhere; it said: "You're feeling overwhelmed because you're doing lots of little insignificant things so you won't have to do the really hard ones that actually matter."

And I was like, "Whoa! Where did *that* come from?"

By refusing to give up, even when meditation seemed bogus, I was able to get in touch with something far beyond my practical, everyday mindset. It's that thing called your soul. Ever since that monumental starting point, I have never stopped inquiring.

The biggest reason meditation is so effective
is that by teaching you about yourself,
it makes you want to keep learning.

Meditation, like anything worthwhile, is not easy. So beating yourself up if you're not able to master it in under five minutes is not the way to go. Be patient with and kind to yourself! Meditation is your time for *you*! When you meditate you're making yourself a priority. And when you make yourself a priority you're infusing more balance into your own life and ultimately into the world. As we said in the very beginning, balance is the dream. We like balance. Balance is our friend.

As this chapter ends, let me ask you a question: If our mind is such an incredibly powerful tool, why do so few of us do anything about trying to understand, leverage or, dare I say, master it? Food for thought, as we move on…

Key MEDITATION takeaways:

- There are many different ways to practice meditation or mindfulness. Experiment with various methods until you find the one that works best for you (and there may be more than one).

- Start with focusing on your breathing: "in cold, out warm" or "smell the soup, blow on the soup." If you find yourself in a stressful situation, and you can remove yourself, go into another room (right before you "fall off the cliff"), and take 10 deep breaths.

- Speak more slowly. When you become more conscious of your speech patterns, your pacing, and the words you choose, you feel more empowered and in control.

- The most important thing you can do is to *not* beat yourself up when your mind goes to thought. Just *gently* bring yourself back to the breath. It's called the *practice* of meditation for a reason!

OPTIMISM

Good Thoughts I Will Find

It's the oldest adage in the book: "Is the glass half empty, or half full?" Well, I hate to be the one to poke a hole in this investigation, but plot twist: It's both. The real question here is not which side you see, but rather on which side you *choose* to focus. That's right, it's a choice! When we start looking at our thoughts as choices, everything changes.

I AM NOT MY THOUGHTS

Remember my tomahawk moment after reading Wayne Dyer's book? The section he wrote on the power of thought really stood out for me, because I suddenly realized that all of the thinking that I was doing — all of that incessant 24/7 mind-churning insanity — was being generated by my own mind! Following that paradigm shift, I was suddenly capable of separating myself from my thoughts and looking at them as an outsider. (And, let me tell you, it wasn't pretty.) I sat in my kitchen and literally said out loud, "Wow, for a 'really good person,' you're pretty damn judgmental!" Up until that moment, I was judging everyone and everything, even myself… without realizing it! And therein lay the problem.

As girls and women, we tend to think a tremendous amount. And, let's face it, most of those thoughts are not about rainbows and unicorns. When we think too much, meaning when we're inside our heads, we sacrifice our sense of awareness. Don't get me wrong, thinking is good, but everything is better in moderation. If we actually believed all the crazy thoughts milling around in our brains, we would probably check ourselves into a mental institution. The first step to curbing our incessant internal debates is *to notice them*. We must consistently check in on what's going on in our noggins, so that we can familiarize ourselves with our thought patterns, and act accordingly. The more we pay attention to the way our thoughts function, the more we understand how to keep them in check. Also, take note of how I said "curbing" and not "stopping." You'll never be able to stop the thoughts entirely — and that's okay! Perfection doesn't exist; only progress does. It's all about learning how to work with what you've got.

Self-awareness is a difficult skill to master for a variety of reasons. The most pervasive reason is our tendency to value ourselves based on the outside world. Being complimented, receiving good grades, getting invited to parties, having 147 billion followers on social media… these are the criteria that boost our self-image.

We care more about what *others* think about us than what *we* think about ourselves. Doesn't that seem backwards? The problem with these external validations is that they're only temporary self-esteem boosters; we deserve something more permanent.

> If your sense of worth is dependent on people and situations external to you, you're not living from the inside-out.

STINKY THINKING 101

Let's say you stub your toe. Naturally, your mind zeroes in on the stubbed toe and how much it hurts. The pain seems to get worse and worse, until it *kills*. Oh, the agony. It's all over. R.I.P. toe.

Here's a novel idea: choose to put your focus on something else. Anything else. Here's a proven scientific fact: your brain can't focus on two things at the exact same time. So the next time you stub your toe, just look up and put all of your attention on the first thing you see. I'm serious. If you look up and see a doorknob, look intently at it and repeat the word "doorknob" over and over again in your head. This sounds weird, but it works! And it just goes to show you, there's another way. There's always another way.

The stubbed toe is a small example, but it speaks significantly to the power of our minds. Our minds can generate some pretty mean thoughts about ourselves and about others. So if, for example, we say to ourselves that we're ugly, fat, or stupid — and we keep thinking about it — the thought becomes bigger and stronger until it takes over.

But when we're aware that we're taking part in what I call "stinky thinking," we have the opportunity to see it for what it is and change it. When you practice monitoring your thoughts, you can say, "Oh, there I go again," and you can begin to choose to replace the stinky thought with one that serves you better. We deserve to be treated well and it all starts with us. Remember: we teach people how to treat us. If we treat ourselves like crap, why would we expect anyone else to treat us any better? It's a big fat "duh," but somehow we all still do it.

Think of a time (possibly just a few minutes ago) when you generated some "stinky thinking." Let's use a generic example:

"Ugh, I hate my thighs. They are so gross. I can't believe I ate another piece of bread. I'm such a loser."

If you were to say out loud to someone else what you just said to yourself, you'd probably think you were one of the nastiest people on the planet. This is what it would sound like:

"Ugh, your thighs are so gross. I can't believe you ate another piece of bread. You're such a loser."

Here's another common example:

"I'm such an idiot. I always say stupid things. What the hell's wrong with me? No wonder I don't have a boyfriend. I'm going to end up alone, living in a tiny wooden shack with 65 cats."

If you were to say this to someone else, they would hear:

"You're such an idiot. You always say stupid things. What the hell's wrong with you? No wonder you don't have a boyfriend. You're going to end up alone, living in a tiny wooden shack with 65 cats."

Would you *ever* say these things to anyone else unprovoked? Of course not! Why, then, do we let ourselves get away with being so mean to ourselves? Living from the inside-out actually forces you to recognize that you have a relationship with yourself. Do your best to make it a good one, just like you would with a friend, colleague, or family member. At the end of the day, your relationship with yourself is the most important one there is.

Take the time to actually hear what you say to yourself and you might just have your very own tomahawk moment.

CATCH AND REPLACE

Getting back to the thought replacement technique: the next time you're doing "stinky thinking" of any kind, remember to catch yourself and simply replace the negative thought with another more helpful thought. In the first example, it might sound something like this:

"Okay, so I ate another slice of bread. And yes, it was awesome. But I made a commitment to myself to eat more healthfully and I broke it. I try not to break commitments to others, so I shouldn't break the ones I make to myself. I'm going to do better next time."

In the second example, it might sound like:

"Wow, I was really nervous talking to Michael. But maybe whatever I said isn't as bad as I'm imagining. I just need to be myself. If he likes me for that, great. If not, I'll meet someone else who does."

STINKY THINKING 201

Now let's take this one step further. It's important to keep in mind that whatever overwhelms us is not usually just about our thinking. Thinking speaks to logic and reason, and those are important. That said, we are emotional, sentient beings; we are designed to feel. And thus, we encounter the second half of the "stinky thinking" equation: our emotions. A thought on its own would not get us riled up; it's the feeling associated with the thought that really puts us over the edge. On the flipside, however, a positive thought married with a positive emotion can instantly improve your mindset in a big way. Remember, you are the captain of your own ship, The SS Consciousness! Don't steer it into an iceberg and let Leo DiCaprio drown.

SEE IT IN YOUR MIND'S EYE

So how do we link our thoughts and feelings to make them work for us? In a word: visualization. Hopefully, through reading these chapters, you're starting to tap into just how amazing your mind is, as well as all its crazy shenanigans. Visualization is one of many empowering skills that we, as conscious human beings, possess. When used consistently and properly, visualization can shift your consciousness like nobody's business. Here's a really cool example to prove it:

A few years ago, scientists did an experiment with an Olympic runner in which they attached electrodes to his calf muscles and then attached them to an EMG (electromyography) machine. They told the runner to visualize running the 100-meter dash. This runner had done visualizations before, so it was second nature for him to put himself in that exact scenario. As the runner was visualizing himself running the race, the EMG machine detected activity from the electrodes attached to the runner's calves and subsequently generated readings as though he were actually running the race. But he was standing totally still! Amazing, right?

Obviously, visualization is not just for athletes. It's for anyone who wants to accomplish something or shift her current circumstance. As you continue reading this book, you'll see that some skills overlap. For example, meditation and visualization are a match made in heaven. You can even do both in the same sitting! Use meditation to focus on your breathing and get yourself out of your head, and then use visualization to clearly bring into focus a goal you want to accomplish or a character trait you want to work on.

When visualizing, it's important to remember to create as detailed a scenario as you can in your mind's eye. In the example of the Olympic runner, he wasn't only imagining his legs moving, but he was imagining the sound of the crowd, sweat on his brow, sound of his sneakers hitting the ground, step by step. I'm talking about really feeling like you're there in that moment. Of course your visualized action doesn't have to be as physically intense as sprinting in the Olympics. It can be as simple as taking a test, confronting a friend about a problem, or learning a new song on the guitar. The most important thing to keep in mind is that the ultimate goal of visualization is not to *trick* yourself into feeling accomplished without taking action — it's to *actually* take action! Yes, dream about answering those hard questions, talking to your friend, or strumming those chords... but then go make some flashcards, pick up the phone, or break out the sheet music!

When you visualize your goal, make it
as real in your mind's eye as possible.

Visualization offers us clarity, which often leads to a heightened sense of motivation... but afterwards, we still need to get up and make it happen.

MUSIC TAMES THE BEAST WITHIN

Visualization is a highly effective tool that produces tangible results, but sometimes we need a little extra push to tap into the mind power that will get us there. One of the things that can get you there in a heartbeat also happens to be one of my favorite subjects — music! Take a moment and think about one of your favorite songs. When it's playing, no matter where you are or what you're doing, you're immediately transported to another emotional state. As a professional songwriter, I know firsthand the impact that music can have, and for that reason, I believe that it's an extremely underutilized tool. When

I'm in a crappy mood, the first thing I do is get my phone and pull up a playlist I created named "Cheer Up."

Music is the universal language and the universal healer.

Music can literally change your body chemistry. It activates both emotional and intellectual regions of the brain, releases dopamine (the feel-good hormone), lowers cortisol levels (the stress hormone), and generally reduces your overall level of anxiety almost instantly. We asked hundreds of girls (aged 11-17) what they do to relieve stress, and listening to music was the number one answer!

With that in mind, I put together a list of some great songs, and included it in the back of this book. The list is divided into eight sections, and each song was handpicked to reinforce the specific lesson taught in that particular chapter. For example, this chapter is "Optimism," so the songs in that section are all about thoughts, visualization, and positivity: Corinne Bailey Rae's "Put Your Records On," R. Kelly's "I Believe I Can Fly," and Pharrell's "Happy," among others.

START TODAY

Here's the bottom line, gals: you wouldn't be mean to others, so don't be mean to yourself. Anger, judgment, and blame are never going to solve problems, but kindness, understanding, and appreciation always will. When all is said and done, every minute you spend chastising yourself is a minute totally wasted! We all have different ways of handling issues — and whatever your way is, *that's okay*. Let today be the day that you decide to be more tolerant of yourself and others (a perfect segue as we move into the next chapter).

Key OPTIMISM takeaways:

- Notice your stinky thinking. Remember that just noticing is a *huge* step. When you do, immediately replace the thought you have with another thought and repeat it a few times. Even if you don't believe it right away, continue to do it until it becomes second nature.

- Visualization is a great way to start your day. Imagine who you want to be and what you want to do, whether it's a tangible, physical goal, or a personality trait you're working on honing. Keep thinking about it, feeling it, and most importantly, taking action toward it. Thinking positive + feeling positive + acting positive = MAGIC!

- Make a playlist with all the songs that make you feel good and listen to it for at least 10 minutes each day.

TOLERANCE

To everyone be kind

O nce upon a time, there was a little boy named Abrum. Abrum lived in a small farm village in Poland called Radich, with his mother Henya, father Akiva, and little sister Manya. Abrum had a wonderful childhood growing up on the farm located at the foothills of the Carpathian Mountains surrounded by strawberry and blueberry patches, apple trees, and a beautiful stream where he and his sister would play. Sounds like a little slice of heaven, doesn't it?

When Abrum was five years old, his parents, who valued education above all, sent him to a school on a horse and buggy about two hours away. He would stay there during the week and come home on the weekends. He missed home terribly, but his parents always stressed to him how important it was for him to get a good education.

On August 2, 1942, when Abrum was just 14 years old, his life changed forever.

On that day, as World War II raged on in full force, his mother, father, and sister were told to report to the nearby town of Turka to be given work relocation instructions. Abrum's mother asked him to stay and watch the farm, and told him they would be back later in the day.

He never saw them again.

When Abrum's family arrived in town, they were shoved onto a cattle car, and shipped off to a death camp where they were immediately killed. Abrum was spared because his mother had the foresight to secure an "arbeiter" (worker) card for him. He knew how to read and write; most people in the village did not. Quite literally, education saved his life.

Soon after, the Nazis came for him, and he escaped deep into the Carpathian Mountains where he lived for the next two years. During that time, Abrum survived the impossible. He was often near starvation, but he fought through. Once, he was captured, but he escaped. On several occasions he was shot at, but each time they missed.

The war ended in 1945 and four years later, on March 17, 1949, he arrived in New York. He had nothing: no family, no job, and no money. He put himself through school, worked odd jobs, and graduated cum laude with an Accounting degree from Baruch College. He eventually started his own firm, got married, and had three children and five grandchildren. All three of his children have made it a priority to continue passing on his incredible story.

I should know. I'm one of them.

DADDY'S GIRL

My father is one of the most inspiring people I know. He's my real-life superhero! He went to hell and back, lost everything that was near and dear to him, and still managed to survive physically *and* maintain an exceptionally positive attitude throughout his entire life. I'm in awe of the man.

My father has told us (his children) many times that it was his mother who saved his life, in more ways than one. She provided him not only with the worker card that kept him from being taken on that fateful day, but with the love and strength that sustained him throughout his life. I share my father's story not only to highlight the importance of tolerance in our world, but also to pay tribute to my grandmother, a true maternal role model. It was her kindness, care, and forethought that saved my father's life — and ultimately gave me mine. I am filled with pride knowing that I am her granddaughter.

For all the moms out there, please take a moment to be grateful that you, at this moment, actually have the privilege of being a mother. The challenge of raising children is unquestionable — but when life becomes difficult or overwhelming, think about Henya. Think about what she and my father wouldn't give to have the chance to be together again as a family.

INTOLERANCE IN OUR OWN BACKYARDS

As the Holocaust becomes a more and more distant memory, I want to ensure that my dad's story is not relegated to a history book and otherwise forgotten. So many people endured unspeakable pain, suffering, loss, and tragedy solely because they were Jewish. *That was the only reason.* But if you know about the Holocaust, you know that the Jews were not the only ones targeted. Hitler and his army had plans to eradicate anyone who was not of the Aryan race, the "master race" of blonde-haired, blue-eyed, Caucasian, purebred Europeans. That could never happen again in this day and age… right?

Wrong. Intolerance has persisted through the decades, leading to countless more mass genocides, such as the ones that took place in Serbia, Rwanda, Bosnia, Sierra Leone, Darfur, and even downtown Manhattan on 9/11. Today, as I write this book, global terrorist organizations continue to spread hatred and violence against those who do not believe as they do. Every act of terrorism serves as a painful reminder of how much more we need to do as a global community to counteract the rampant intolerance that permeates our world.

We can all understand how horrific these things are on a global scale, but do we ever stop to think about it on a local scale? In our communities? Our schools? Our families? Intolerance is intolerance — period. Any form of it is dangerous and should be treated as such. Think about the bully on the playground who disparages other children because of their weight, height, skin color, clothes, and even religious beliefs. If that bully's actions were addressed with the same sense of horror that global intolerance elicits, the chances of another mass genocide would nearly be eliminated.

There are dozens of stereotypes that perpetuate intolerance: gender, race, sexual orientation, religion, culture, etc. However, if you're observant, you'll know that human intolerance is not limited to these larger categories. Both consciously and subconsciously, we put others down for the smallest of things — things a person has no control over — such as a birthmark, their height, the way they walk, talk, chew their food… the list is never-ending. It's no wonder there's so much hatred in our world. We're trying to combat hate with hate! It's a total recipe for disaster.

Adding to the list of bad news is the fact that intolerance is harder than ever to address, thanks to the boundless technologies that govern our society. Cyber-bullying is much more difficult to control because the internet is so easily accessible and spreads information like wildfire. Once a hurtful remark is posted, shared, or messaged, it's now out there with the potential to end up on every screen used by humankind. And by allowing that to happen, we're being anything *but* kind.

When you use your cell phone to blame,
shame or embarrass someone, it says
more about *you* than your target.

Somehow, when we see the grotesque manifestations of inhumanity played out through war and atrocity, it's crystal clear to us how wrong it is — but when we see it played out right in front of us on a mobile device, it merits no more than a shrug. Technology has granted us the "permission" to trash our peers without having to say it to their faces; but that permission has done nothing more than create a bunch of cowards. It's time we realized that it's the "smaller" instances of intolerance of which we need to be most mindful. Just as smoldering embers left unattended have the ability to spread into a massive, devastating fire, so too can bits of intolerance snowball into an unimaginable Holocaust.

Girls, do you speak up when you see injustice playing out in front of you? Do you alert an adult when things get out of hand? Women, how about you? Are you calling out the wrongdoers, or are you tacitly going along with their judgment, trying not to make any waves?

The next time you choose to not say or do anything in the face of intolerance, just remember: if you're not part of the solution, you're part of the problem.

THE ORIGINS OF HATRED

I often ask myself why there is so much hatred and intolerance in the world. How did this come to be? This may seem like a complex question, but in all honesty the answer is pretty straightforward. Outward intolerance is merely a reflection of what's going on inside. Our negativity toward others originates in our own insecurities, and we project those internal conflicts onto the external world. If we're intolerant of ourselves, how we can we possibly be tolerant of others? As American surfer Laird Hamilton said, "Make sure your worst enemy doesn't live between your own two ears." By the same token, however, if we make a conscious choice to be kind to ourselves, we'd be amazed at our capacity for kindness toward the rest of the world.

We can't have peace in *the* world until
we have peace in our *own* world.

INTOLERANCE PART I: BE AWARE, DON'T COMPARE

One major way we convince ourselves of our lack of worth is by comparing ourselves to others. The comparison game is poisonous. It's a surefire way to sabotage our relationship with the person who *should* be our best friend: ourselves. Here's the eye-opening thing about the comparison game — we tend to only compare the parts of our lives where we feel a lack. Girls might look at attractive celebrities and say "Oh, if only my body looked like that!", or "Oh, if only I had their talent!" The problem with that line of thinking is if you're going to compare your life to someone else's, you need to compare your *whole* life to their *whole* life.

The truth is, we have no idea what goes on behind closed doors in another person's day-to-day existence.

On the surface, you might see someone with lots of success, money, beauty, and popularity. But what if you found out that that person has an eating disorder? Or maybe has a toxic relationship with her parent? Or is being stalked by a creepy, potentially dangerous fan? What if you knew all that? Would you still want to swap places with them? My guess is… no, thanks! In fact, they might even want to switch places with *you*! Never thought about it that way, did you?

> Don't compare your life to someone else's. Compare it to the best version of the life you want to live.

The healthier, non-stinky thinking way is to be a racehorse. Yes, a racehorse. Racehorses wear blinders when they race, so they can focus on the path ahead without being distracted by their competitors. You need to do the same. Put on your blinders and focus on your own route, your own gifts, and your own potential. The comparison game is exhausting, both mentally and physically. Don't give in to it! (Girls, don't think this is only directed at you. Moms are just as guilty of playing the comparison game as you are.)

If we take even the smallest step toward catching ourselves when we start measuring our lives against someone else's, and then consciously choose to wear those racehorse blinders, we are making huge strides for tolerance. And look, if you're going to compare, compare yourself to the best possible version of *you*! Because, remember, if we all threw our problems in a pile and had the option to take someone else's, we'd grab ours back in a heartbeat.

INTOLERANCE PART 2: TAUGHT TO HATE?

It's amazing how many times I've encountered women who talk about their relationship with their own mother, swearing up and down that they will never be like them or do to their kids what their mom did to them. Yet somehow, the patterns continue. Unless we wake up and smell the hummus, we're bound to repeat some of our unconscious behaviors when raising our own kids.

Moms, think about how you were raised. How did your mom talk about herself? Did she use disparaging words or accepting ones? How did she talk about others? Did she trash talk her neighbors, coworkers, or family members? How did she treat you? Did she encourage, compliment, and instill pride in you? Or did she tend to embarrass, malign, and belittle you?

Be careful — our daughters absorb, both consciously and unconsciously, every word we say about others and ourselves.

Now, think about how you feel about yourself as an adult and as a mom. How do you talk about yourself? Do you use disparaging words or accepting ones? How do you talk about others? Do you trash talk your neighbors, coworkers, or family members? How do you treat your kids? Do you encourage, compliment, and instill pride in them? Or do you tend to embarrass, malign, and belittle them? Do you notice a connection?

Just as you listened intently to every word out of your mother's mouth, so too our daughters are listening to us. They're walking sponges and they're taking it all in. If you've struggled with self-esteem, today can be the first day you decide to change your mind. Do it for yourself *and* your daughter. We all want our daughters to value, respect, and love themselves. If that's what you want for them, then you need to first give that gift to yourself.

This self-loathing many of us suffer from is not entirely our own fault. Many of us were taught to be self-critical. Heredity, the media, our individual experiences, and the people around us have influenced our perceptions, beliefs, and actions from day one. But it's not helpful to blame those external forces. Ultimately, it's up to us to counteract those influencers. It's up to us to reprogram our minds.

If being intolerant of ourselves is taught, then it must be learned... and if it's learned, then it can be *unlearned*. The sooner we start unlearning, the better.

EDUCATING THE WHOLE CHILD

For those of us who have already learned intolerance, unlearning is our next step. But what about the next generation? What about our kids, who are only just beginning their journeys of self-discovery? If we want to see progress made on the issue of intolerance in our lifetime, we must also rethink how we educate our children in school. Current character education programs don't even scratch the surface of the changes we need to make. These programs are like a Band-Aid on a gaping wound. We can't just put up inspiring quotes in the hallways and expect children to learn empathy. We can't hold one assembly on multiculturalism and expect kids to wholly embrace their classmates' unfamiliar backgrounds. We can't demand that a child who's yelled a racial slur at another child write a formal apology and expect that they'll be discouraged from doing it again. These tactics simply do not work. We need to develop, test, and model a more robust, engaging, and interactive curriculum that cultivates all aspects of what it means to be a human being — one that is focused not merely on academia, but on social and emotional awareness as well.

This concept of teaching *the whole child* through Social Emotional Learning (SEL) has been around for over 20 years and has been slowly expanding and growing. According to CASEL (The Collaborative for Academic, Social, and Emotional Learning), SEL is "a curriculum that teaches mental skills that lead to understanding and managing emotion, setting positive realistic goals, building long-lasting relationships, showing empathy for others, and problem-solving constructively and ethically." SEL teaches our children how to be human beings first and foremost, so they can cultivate the self-control, compassion, and an ability to get along with other people who might not think, talk, or behave like they do. Imagine that! Maybe learning to be a good person should actually take precedence over learning to memorize facts and figures or sit through a standardized test!

If we don't start teaching our children tolerance and empathy, we'll end up with a planet full of highly educated jerks.

While it's important to acknowledge and welcome new ways of educating children in our schools, it's paramount to remember that home is the first and most important "school" for our children. Home is the foundation. Home is where the seeds are planted. Modeling empathy, gratitude, mindfulness, self-esteem, flexibility, tolerance, and love is a parent's job. Put some thought into preparing the curriculum you want your children to graduate from!

Of course, the best of both worlds happens when schools and parents effectively partner together to create a robust and collaborative program. So speak up, get involved, and take action! And check out additional resources in the "Resources/Websites" section in the back of the book.

TOLERANCE AS A THRESHOLD

An alternate definition of tolerance is "the ability to accept, experience, or survive something harmful or unpleasant," such as a high tolerance for pain. Having a high tolerance threshold is often looked upon as a good thing. But as I've gotten older (and wiser), I've realized that there have been many occasions where I tolerated something I shouldn't have. What happens when our tolerance is *too* high?

Girls, why do you allow boys to make inappropriate, offensive, and borderline obscene comments about you? Why do you let your so-called "friends" talk down to you over trivial situations? Why do you permit teachers to treat you unfairly when you work so hard day in and day out? Are you afraid of how you'll be perceived if you speak up? Do the boys' comments make you feel popular or desirable? Do you feel like it's not worth the effort to stand up to other girls and risk ending up friendless? Does it put your grades in jeopardy to question an authority figure? Whatever the case may be, when someone says something that makes you feel uncomfortable or upset, you have every right to respond and make it clear that you will *not* tolerate it. A simple yet firm "don't speak to me like that" will let them know what you will and will not put up with.

You may find that taking that first step might be directed to some in your own family. I'm sure there are times where you feel like you've tolerated too much B.S., where you feel like you just give and give and give and it's not reciprocated.

There have been times when I, Sheira, "Princess of Empowerment," have reached my limit and gone over the edge. Times where I've kept my cool until some attitude gets hurled my way triggering an explosion: "LISTEN YOU *#@&!!!!! I DO EVERYTHING FOR THIS FAMILY AND YOU HAVE THE FREAKIN' NERVE TO TALK TO ME LIKE THAT?! ONE MORE WORD AND I'LL TAKE THIS ENTIRE PLATE OF PASTA THAT I JUST SLAVED OVER FOR AN HOUR AND THROW IT IN YOUR UN-GRATEFUL FREAKIN' FACE!" (More of a mom example, but girls, I'm sure you can relate too.)

We've all been there. Now, I know what you're thinking: *Sheira, what happened to tolerance?* To that I say: sometimes having that instinctive, visceral reaction helps you identify what you're willing to tolerate. Once you get in touch with this, you can move forward in a less hostile way (more on that in Chapter 6). It's situations like the one above that help us establish standards for ourselves. When we start channeling our priorities, living from the inside-out, and putting ourselves first, we elevate our self-worth. That, in turn, has an affect on those around us and ultimately, creates a ripple effect in our families, social circles, and communities.

With every word and action we take, we are teaching people how to treat us.

Have you ever heard of the "Butterfly Effect"? Meteorologist Edward Lorenz realized that the flapping of one butterfly's wings on one side of the hemisphere could create tiny changes in the atmosphere that lead to violent weather conditions elsewhere on the planet. We simply can't predict how making one small shift in our lives will impact the world around us. So when it comes to living this way, you have my permission to be *self*-ish.

THE HAPPY IDIOT

That's my husband's ever-so-loving nickname for me. It's probably because I choose to see the good in people, circumstances, and life as much as possible. The running joke in my family is that "if you put Sheira in a pile of cow manure, she'll tell you how good it is for your skin." It might sound silly, but you know what? I'm ok with it.

When I look at a stranger on the street, all I see is a human being, just like me. I see a person with a heart, brain, and body — just like me. They could be male or female, young or old, short or tall, thin or heavy, gay or straight, black, white, yellow, brown or purple; it doesn't matter. I see a person with wants, needs, emotions, experiences, and every other aspect that's universal to the human race.

Furthermore, I see how I play a role in their life simply by interacting with them, even if only once. And I don't take this role lightly. I think we need more happy idiots on our planet — people who see no place for hatred, intolerance, shame, or blame. Everyone is simply doing the best they can with what they've been given — and if we internalize that, we will be left with no reason to hate anyone or anything.

We are all born loving, kind, giving, and tolerant beings. From birth on we're all taught, raised, and influenced by our different upbringings — but that doesn't take away from the fact that we're all born with the same blank slate. My dad taught me the importance of being tolerant, even when the world isn't — a lesson he learned from his beautiful, loving, and kind-hearted mother. My wish for us gorgeous girls and women is that we endow every word, action, and intention with love and care for others and ourselves. Make a choice today to not allow any room in your life for hatred, resentment, or intolerance. Not for strangers on the street, not for your co-workers not for your family, and certainly not for yourself. In the words of Dr. Martin Luther King Jr., "Darkness cannot drive out darkness. Only light can do that. Hate cannot drive out hate; only love can do that." If we do this on a consistent basis, the torch will be passed on to future generations of girls... and the memory of my grandmother, Henya Brayer, will live on.

I'd like to share the lyrics to one of my songs, which was inspired by my father's journey. I don't want to get too "Kumbaya" on you, but I believe that one of the reasons I was put on this planet is to help move the world away from fear and towards connection. I hope it inspires you to see the world through a new set of eyes.

We're All The Same
© Sheira Brayer

"We're All The Same" is available on most digital platforms including iTunes and Spotify.

I often stop and wonder where we get all our thunder
When will the vicious cycle end?
I cannot seem to understand why man is inhumane to man
When will we call each other 'friend'?

CHORUS:
Cause we're all the same; we laugh and cry
We're all the same; we all live and die
Let's make the journey matter now
Let's win the game
We're all the same; when cut we bleed
We're all the same; we all have a need
To love and to be loved and to let peace reign
We're all the same

We've got so much to live for, picture a world without war
Put all the hatred in the past
This would make quite a story to leave our children glory
The kind of glory that will last

CHORUS

Look at your neighbor, and think of what would happen
If danger came to our world
Wouldn't care about race or color
No, we'd be side by side with each other
Just like sister and brother
Oh can't you see how it could be?

Cause we're all the same; we laugh and cry
We're all the same; we all live and die
Let's make the journey matter now
Let's win the game

We're all the same under the skin
We're all the same deep down within
Want to be proud of who we are
Not be ashamed

We're all the same; gonna make it real
We're all the same; now let's start to heal
And take responsibility instead of blame

We're all the same; oh can't you feel it
We're all the same; if we could only see it
Then we'd have everything in the world to gain

Cause we're all the same
We're all the same
After all we're all the same

Key TOLERANCE takeaways:

- Tolerance starts within. You can't give away what you don't have inside. Start noticing your "stinky thinking" when it comes to tolerating yourself, and over time you'll see how much more you have to give to others.

- If you witness intolerance of any kind, speak up. It doesn't have to be long and preachy. A simple "Hey, what you're doing isn't right" may be enough to get someone else to take notice. That said, never put yourself or others in harm's way. Call for help if you feel a situation may escalate and put you or someone else in danger.

- Notice behavior from others that you tolerate that maybe you shouldn't. Put boundaries in place for what doesn't feel right to you (verbally and physically). It's a critical step in empowering yourself.

- Pay it forward! Do a random act of kindness every day or volunteer your time to a great organization — it costs nothing and feels amazing!

Following are several photos that provide background about my dad's life, and help frame his journey from Poland to the United States… and back again.

This is the youngest photo I have of my dad (age 16). It was taken right after the war.

This is the only picture my dad has of his family. On the left is his mother, Henya and on the right, his little sister Manya.

In 2009, after many years of begging my dad, we finally made the journey back to Poland and found his house.

The trip was one of the most emotional experiences of my life.

My dad standing in front of his house overlooking the hill where he and his sister used to play.

INTUITION

When I'm in a bind

I HAVE A.D.D.

O ver the past few years, I've slowly been contracting adult-onset A.D.D. In this case, however, A.D.D. does not stand for Attention Deficit Disorder — it stands for Addictive Devices Disease. If you don't think that having those digital dings, pings, and rings around 24/7/365 is a disease or an addiction, you're quite mistaken. Digital addiction is on the rise, recognized by scientists, educators, and doctors alike. Social media, texting, and the endless stream of apps that dominate our daily activity have all combined to create a thick layer of detachment — not only between ourselves and others, but between ourselves and our own intuition.

Intuition is potentially the single most critical ability we possess. Sadly, it's also the one we tend to ignore the most. Intuition is our gut feeling — that little voice inside that whispers to us telling us which way to go. It's not something derived by conscious reasoning; rather, it's a product of our unadulterated human instinct. It's our very own internal GPS system.

So… if we're ignoring our own GPS system, won't we get lost?

Yes; yes we will. It's okay to be lost, confused, and directionless sometimes. Often it's the best way to realize how truly resilient we are. But we must recognize that in order to get back on track we have to listen to our intuition. That said, acknowledging its existence is only half the battle. Once we locate our intuition, we need to learn to trust it. Just as our bodies heal our cuts and wounds, so too does our intuition point us toward the answers to life's most difficult situations.

But first we need to be quiet and listen.

INTUITION IN THE REAL WORLD

Imagine that you're taking a multiple-choice test and you're grappling between two answers. Your first inclination is to pick choice (a), but then you think about choice (c) again, and rationalize that it might be (c). Your gut, however, keeps going back to (a). You go back and forth a few times and finally put down (c) as your answer. When you get the test back you kick yourself because you see that the right answer was, in fact... (a).

Start using your intuition for the smaller decisions in your life. The more you practice listening, the better you'll get at it.

That's just a small example to which we can all relate... but what about when it's something important? What about when you have to make decisions that have more critical consequences?

I think I feel a story coming on!

MY FIRST ENCOUNTER WITH MARY-JUANA

When I was in 10th grade, a gorgeous 11th grader named Adam asked me out. Adam was the ultimate TDH (tall, dark, and handsome). His dimples and great sense of humor really sealed the deal. So when he invited me to go to a Billy Joel concert at Madison Square Garden, I was OUT OF MY MIND excited! But as I approached the platform of the train station where we agreed to meet, he was standing there with two other guys. He hadn't mentioned anything about bringing his friends. I was pretty bummed, but I went along anyway.

Then, 15 minutes into the concert, as I was belting "Summer Highland Falls" at the top of my lungs, I noticed a small white stick making its way toward my face. It was, as you may have guessed, a joint. I had never tried any drugs or alcohol before and wasn't about to now. As Adam and his friends continued insisting that I try it, I felt more and more uncomfortable saying "No, thank you" to them. My thoughts were like a scene out of a cartoon where the devil is sitting on one shoulder and an angel on the other:

"What's the big deal? It won't kill you. Just try it!"

"Yeah, but I've never done it before, and I don't know these guys that well. What if it does something weird to me and I pass out?"

"Well, if you try it, Adam will think you're cool and maybe this could turn into something! Look how cute he is!"

"But it doesn't feel right. It's illegal for G-d's sake! What if there are policemen around and they catch me and I end up in jail? I look awful in stripes!"

The good news: That small voice in my head was getting pretty loud and with a final emphatic "No!", they stopped. The bad news: The rest of the night was really awkward — probably because they were high and I wasn't. Sad to say, I never got a second chance with Adam. He really was so damn cute.

It's interesting for me to think back on that night and realize that the decision I made was the result of my intuition at work. Unfortunately, I wasn't aware of it back then. If I had been, I would have tapped into it a lot more in my young adult life when I made some really stupid decisions based on what other people said, thought, and felt.

DECLUTTERING YOUR SOUL

The Adam "date" was a tough situation for me at the time, but girls today have a lot more to deal with than I did when I was a teen. Back in the day, the only media outlets we had access to (or I should say, had access to us) were movies, television, radio, and magazines. Today, millions of messages are being hurled at us at light speed via Instagram, Snapchat, Twitter, Tumblr, Facebook, Pinterest, YouTube, digital billboards and a kajillion websites (thousands are created every minute)! And, to be honest, a lot of the information out there in Digitaland is inappropriate, confusing, and sometimes just plain false. It's almost impossible to navigate it all and maintain your sanity.

The key to staying true to yourself in a world full of noise?

Listening to your intuition.

You need to ensure that your own voice is louder than anything that's making its way into your periphery. These days, it's far too easy to get sucked into the black hole of technology. As you press, tap, click, and swipe hours can go by without you even knowing it. In a very literal sense, your device is a drug that's luring you to an altered mind state. You must have control over your technology — not the other way around. Slavery ended in 1865, people!

Technology is supposed to serve us,
not enslave us.

THE BOILING FROG

Addiction of any kind is hard to identify. When it comes to drugs, alcohol, food, sex, gambling, exercise, and, yes, mobile devices we're not necessarily aware that we're addicted because addiction tends to start slowly and build over time. You may be able to relate through the following  metaphor known as "The Boiling Frog." Scientists placed a frog in boiling water and it immediately jumped out of the pot. However, when it was placed in cold water that was slowly heated, it didn't perceive the danger and was slowly cooked to death.

This metaphor represents the inability or unwillingness of people to react to change that occurs gradually. This is critical for any parent who's contemplating giving — no, *gifting* — their daughter with a digital device. Beforehand, if you showed her a video of someone who walked around glued to their device every second of every day she would probably be a bit alarmed. However, once you give her such a device, chances are you will find her using it more and more and more… until eventually she won't be able to leave it out of her sight! She'll slowly turn into one of those people whose technology becomes a permanent fixture on their body — and that's when you know you may have a problem.

To avoid the materialization of this scenario, talk to your daughter about the dangers of digital addiction, set some boundaries, and most importantly model the behavior you want from her. I can't tell you how many adults I know who are truly addicted to technology! Think of the message you're sending to your child by taking their phone away for excessive usage when you use yours just as much or more. Like any other addiction, use can turn to abuse over time if you're not paying attention! I know how much self-control is required to unplug — but trust me, it's worth it.

By the way, www.virtual-addiction.com is a website that has a 12-question quiz to determine whether you're suffering from digital addiction. It will tell whether you should disconnect from your devices — either partially or altogether — and, as they put it, "plug back into life!" (The irony is not lost on me that you have to use your computer to find out if you're addicted to your computer... but desperate times call for desperate measures.)

LIFE BEFORE SOCIAL MEDIA

When I present my Motiv8 seminar for mothers and daughters, I ask the girls to imagine their lives without phones, computers, the internet, social media, etc. I then ask them if their lives would be better or worse, and why. It's astonishing — yet refreshing — to know that, on average, 80% of the girls say their lives would be better without technology. When I delve further, they acknowledge that despite its positive aspects (sharing information and pictures, staying connected to friends, making plans, etc.) the stress of always having to be "on," as well as the gossip and the mean-spirited nature that pervade their digital world, can be extremely overwhelming.

We all know that technology is here to stay and, in many ways, it's an incredible tool that makes our lives easier and more efficient. But when it starts to eat away at the essence of who you are, it's no longer serving you. And when something no longer serves you (whether it's a device, a job, or a friendship) you need to find another way to handle it, which sometimes means detoxing for a while. Hey, they have food detoxes (a.k.a. cleanses) — so why not digital detoxes? You'll be amazed at how the world can still function without you being on your cell phone, laptop or iPad!

DEVICES ARE NOT THE ONLY VICES

The digital world certainly contributes to the drowning out of our intuitive voice, but it's not the only culprit. In many instances, other people's opinions are just as responsible for your self-doubt and confusion as any form of media. As well-intentioned as many of the people in your life are, they will never be able to see life through your eyes. Only you can do that. We girls and women tend to value outside opinions when we're facing a dilemma or feeling down. However, while we all can learn a tremendous amount from our fellow women (and men), allowing too many outside voices into our heads doesn't leave much room for our own perspective. It's important that you recalibrate your mental scale so that *your* opinion weighs more than all the others. There's nothing wrong with asking for help, but at some point, you have to say, "Enough outside opinions. I got this!"

Trust yourself. Trust yourself. Trust yourself.

We may not realize it, but we make decisions based on suggestions from friends, colleagues, and family all the time. From small, every-day decisions to major life choices, we allow other people to take up too much real estate in our brain — and they're not even paying us rent! Here are some examples:

"Don't go out with Mark! He's a loser!"

"Take this diet pill. It'll help you lose weight really easily!"

"Don't move to Colorado! You'll be so homesick!"

"You totally should get this pocketbook. It's so much cuter than that one!"

Everyone has their own frame of reference and perspective based on the way they were brought up. Years of their own personal experiences, which have shaped their beliefs, biases, fears, and preferences are now being layered onto your decision. So essentially, the people in your life are telling you what they would do *if they were you*. BUT THEY'RE NOT YOU!

Writer Anais Nin said, "We don't see things as they are. We see them as we are."

The truth is you have a lot more wisdom and strength inside you than you realize. You are beautiful, talented, and worthy just as you are. Of course, you should always feel free to ask for input, suggestions, and advice from the people you trust and respect most. No woman is an island. But also don't forget that you don't *need* other people to make the important decisions of your life. The more you rely on yourself, the happier you'll be.

Bottom (rhyming) line: Listen to your gut… no matter what!

NOW WE'RE GETTING SOMEWHERE

Given that we're four skills deep into the book, it's time to take stock of the bigger picture. Honing your intuition overlaps with the first three skills. When you begin to quiet your mind (Meditation), it allows you to more easily monitor your thoughts (Optimism), which makes you more open to choosing kindness toward yourself and others (Tolerance), which ultimately motivates you to want to further explore your inner workings (Intuition). And when you tap into your intuition (a.k.a. the deepest part of who you are, a.k.a. your truth), you'll be able to make decisions that serve *you* well, that move *you* closer to what *you* enjoy, that add to *your* health, that give *you* more perspective, and that bring *you* peace. Remember that your life is not a dress rehearsal — it's the real thing! You're only given one (unless you're a cat), so live it wisely.

The following are some practical actions that you can start taking today to hone your intuition:

1. *Give yourself a time-out.* All of us can find a few minutes each day to shut everything off, unplug, and breathe. It's amazing what this simple act can do for your quality of life. You also might want to consider implementing a "no devices during mealtime" rule in your home. I implemented it with my family and it has really made a difference. We actually converse with each other now! Crazy, huh?

2. *Don't be so accessible to everyone all the time.* You and you alone set the tone for the communications in your life. If you respond to every text, email, and post the second you receive it, you're setting a precedent and establishing unrealistic expectations for your peers. You're saying to them, "I'm always available" and "Whatever is going on in my life is not as important as your text/email/post." It doesn't bode well for your level of self-respect, your free time, or the most important ingredient for a healthy life: balance. Next time, think twice before you respond immediately. Few things are that urgent that they need to be answered right away.

3. *When you wake up in the morning, say hello to yourself in the mirror.* I know… this sounds weird. But the truth is, many of us have forgotten how to connect with ourselves because we're so invested in our devices and the people around us. So as you're brushing your teeth or putting on your make-up, simply acknowledge the image staring back at you with a quick "Hi" (and a smile, of course). It might seem strange at first, but who knows? You just might make a new friend (which is the whole point of this book)!

4. *Spend some time journaling.* If you want to truly discover what makes you tick, then open a notebook, grab a pen, and write. There's no key on a keyboard that serves as an effective substitute for handwritten communication. I kept a diary for many years and, let me tell you, it's some of the most entertaining pieces of literature I've ever read (and also some of the scariest). In addition to self-connection, it's also tremendously helpful with regard to problem solving. In the face of a dilemma, writing down pros and cons — or best- and worst-case scenarios — will make you feel a lot more in control.

MAKING THE MOST OF YOUR INTUITION

The reason I believe many of us ignore our intuition is that often, what it's telling us to do isn't the easiest or most popular choice. For example, girls: if you're at a party and there are illegal activities going on (smoking, drugs, alcohol, etc.) and you're not feeling comfortable, it's probably because your intuition is saying "Nuh, uh. No good! Don't do it!" However, you still go back and forth in your head because turning your friends down might make them think you're a loser. But when you're living from the inside-out, you have to put yourself first and do what works best for you. If you feel hesitant about doing anything (especially when it comes to putting foreign substances in your body), you have every right to refuse. And if any of your friends look down on your decision, well, that's their problem. Don't make other people's problem your problem. If you choose to succumb to peer pressure and take an illegal substance only to have an adverse reaction or end up becoming addicted and jeopardizing your health, who's going to be there to pick up the pieces? Not them!

Your intuition is your own personal guide
to being the best version of yourself.

Another non-substance-related scenario where you may be ignoring your intuition is witnessing someone being intentionally mistreated. Your gut might be telling you to speak up because you know it's wrong, but you hesitate because if you do speak up, you might get awkward stares of disapproval, or worse — the focus of the hostility might shift to you. Maybe you don't want to take the risk of putting yourself in that situation. But that's what courage is: doing the right thing regardless of how uncomfortable or scary it might be. If that small voice in your head is telling you to simply say "Hey, cut it out!" to the wrongdoers, that's the voice you have to listen to.

A word of caution: if you witness a scene and your gut tells you that this may escalate to violence, make sure to keep yourself safe. There's absolutely nothing wrong with getting a higher authority involved, whether that's a parent, a teacher, or even the police. If you don't and something bad happens, you may never forgive yourself.

Moms, here's an example for you: When you say "No" to your daughter's request to go to a party where there will be no parental supervision, you might experience a lot of backlash. She might put up a huge fight, have a hissy fit, or tell you she hates you. But if you truly believe it's in your daughter's best interest not to go, trust your intuition, and as calmly as you can, explain to her why you've made your ruling and then go about your business. Side note: If your daughter doesn't tell you she hates you at least once during her teen years, it means you're not fulfilling your role as a parent.

Until a girl becomes an adult, her mother's
goal should be to model good behavior;
not to be liked by her daughter.

In today's society, many moms are making decisions based on wanting to be their daughter's friend and earn their approval. But that's not always what being a mom is about. If the need to be "the cool mom" is the determining factor of your parenting decisions, you may want to re-evaluate. At this point in your daughter's life, she doesn't need another buddy. There will be plenty of time to be her friend once you've done your primary job of guiding, advising, disciplining, and educating.

Although it might be nice to have a crystal ball that can see into the future, it would also take the fun, adventure, and joy of self-discovery out of life. Every mistake, challenge, conflict, and meltdown makes you that much more capable of honoring your intuition. If you can look at every negative experience as preparation for more positive ones, you're on your way to a healthier, more fulfilling life.

Something to ponder as we move into the halftime show!

Key INTUITION takeaways:

- That still small voice inside you is your very own built-in GPS system that's always steering you in the right direction. Learn to trust it. It might be rusty from lack of use — but the more you check in with it, the more it will help you break through the noise and clutter in your life.

- Take in the opinions and suggestions of the people you respect, but always make sure your own voice is the one carrying the most weight.

- Listen to your gut! No matter what!

THE HALF TIME SHOW

And now it's time for a short break. Go take a walk, stretch your legs, have a snack... whatever floats your boat.

When you're back, as part of the halftime show entertainment, I'm going to take you on a fun little journey, in a segment I like to call:

SHEIRA'S AWKWARD HAIR:
A Journey Through the Years

There are two reasons I'm sharing this photo gallery with you. The first is, it consistently gets the biggest laughs when I do it in my live Motiv8 program. The second... will be revealed to you soon.

So sit back, relax, and enjoy my awkward hair!

This is me at age 5 (on the left). Everyone, all together now: "Awww!" What kind of crazy hairdo was my mother going for here? Mary-Kate and Ashley Olsen meet Princess Leia from Star Wars?

Here I am in the second grade. Yes folks, my mom gave me that haircut for the sole purpose of my class picture being taken! Take a close look at the bangs, friends. This is the work of a master.

This is one of my faves. My hair looks like it's been crazy glued to my scalp (yup, I'm on the left again). Let me clarify: we are not Amish, we are not going to a costume party and, yes, the necklace I'm wearing has a mouse with a piece of cheese. Somebody, quick, put me on a runway!

This is me at age 12. The hair simply reflects the stage of confusion I was going through at that period of my life. I know I advocate being kind to yourself… but these pictures are too good of an opportunity for some comic relief!

Can you guess what decade this is? Yup, it's the '80s! My hair was not as large and in charge as the hair of some other folks back then; however, if you look closely, you'll see a slight resemblance to…

But wait, there's hope…

This was taken the day I married
my amazing husband, Cory.

Here's why I'm actually sharing these photos with you: We need to stop taking ourselves so seriously! A little less drama; a little more laughter. We're all perfectly imperfect human beings. That's what makes us charming! And, more importantly, we need to remember that everything in life is a phase. Nothing lasts forever, for better or worse. We're always saying hello and goodbye to people, places, and situations. That said, the one constant is *you*. You get to decide how you react to everything that happens to you. And let me tell you, the phases of life just seem to go faster and faster as time goes on. So take my cue and enjoy the ride!

This photo journey takes you through the life of someone who used to live from the outside-in and now lives from the inside-out. And although my external beauty may be starting to fade (some would argue that happened a long time ago), I'd much rather be the strong, self-aware person I am today than the insecure new bride I was back then.

VIBE

Is mine high or low?

WHO IN THE WORLD ARE YOU?

You know how you meet someone, and afterwards you feel like you have a sense of who they are from how they came across? You might say something like "I like that person. I got a good vibe from them." Or contrarily, you might say, "I'm staying away from them. They gave me weird vibes."

What does that mean exactly?

Vibe is short for "vibration." But what does vibration have to do with anything? Well, as it turns out, a lot! We are more magnificent, miraculous, and marvelous than our mere mortal bodies. You may not fully comprehend it right now, but there's a whole other level of cosmic activity going on around you even as we speak. In fact, there is an entire energy field surrounding you. Don't be scared; it won't hurt you.

Quantum physics (a pretty cool branch of physical science) proves that we're all made of the same matter: atoms and molecules. However, and all scientists agree on this fact, when you break things down at a level smaller than atoms and molecules (sub-atomic particles), everything is pure energy. *You* are pure energy. (Whoa, this is getting heavy!)

Actually, it's getting lighter. Because when you realize that everyone is pure energy, it allows you to look at your fellow humans, yourself, and this whole thing we call "life" in a different way. This unified energy field I just referenced surrounds not just us, but every single thing in the universe! Take a look at your sibling, your kitchen table, the moon, a peacock, or a slice of American cheese. They all look incredibly different... and yet, they're all made of the same stuff!

The coolest thing about this omnipresent energy is that it's made up of frequencies — high, low, and everything in between — much like a radio tower. Quantum physics dictates that all frequencies of energy attract similar frequencies... so in order to tune into the station you desire (in your case, the experiences you want to have), you need to be emitting similar frequencies to the ones you're looking to attract.

So if everything in the universe is made up of pure energy, that includes our thoughts! Our thoughts and emotions are constantly pulling us toward the frequency that we're emitting. When our thoughts and emotions are vibrating at higher frequencies, it's associated with corresponding emotions of joy, love, passion, optimism, and enthusiasm. On the opposite end of the spectrum, lower frequencies are associated with sadness, overwhelm, worry, anger, and resentment. And, then there's everything in between — an entire spectrum of frequencies.

Take a minute right now and actually imagine your entire body as an energy field with protons, neutrons, and electrons emanating from you. Watch as they collide, interact, and communicate with the energy fields and frequencies of everyone and everything around you. Visualizing that concept alone can completely shift your awareness about who you are as a miraculous being on this planet!

If you're reading about this phenomenon for the first time, some of you might be thinking it sounds pretty out there. Some of you may be thinking it sounds cool and interesting, and some of you may be contemplating committing me to the loony bin. Any of those reactions is perfectly acceptable. Just keep reading.

KARMA: WHAT YOU GIVE IS WHAT YOU GET

Everyone has heard of karma. Unfortunately, she's usually associated with being a bitch! Personally, I think karma gets a bad rap. If you think about it, she's only a bitch when someone wrongs her first (for example, sends her bad vibes). My feeling is if you believe that what you give is what you get, why not choose to put some deliciously good vibes out into the world? Then karma will probably be a total sweetheart and you can both go get your nails done and be best friends forever!

Karma's only a bitch
when she's wronged.

Many of us unconsciously emit negative energy in the form of criticism, complaints, revenge, jealousy, hatred, and judgment. But if you think for a second that negative energy only affects the person at whom you're directing those emotions, think again. That negativity affects your own inner energy, which then affects your outer energy, and prompts a whole vicious cycle. In the end, it hurts you more than it hurts your target. You can't whine and complain, bitch and moan, kick and scream, and still feel happy inside. It's just not quantum-physically possible. So just focus on your own protons, neutrons, and electrons and don't worry about everyone else's. Your energy is in your control for as long as you choose to be conscious of it.

Now, quick tip of what not to do: don't put "fake" good energy out there just to see what happens. If you fake smile at the waiter when you really want to trip him because your steak was too well done, or if you begrudgingly give money to a charity to see if you get money back somehow, don't bother. Karma's an excellent judge of character. She can read right through that crap. At the end of the day, it all comes down to intention, and she knows it. And so do you.

Back in the chapter on Optimism, we talked about thoughts being choices. It's important to note that the thoughts we generate lead to corresponding emotions, which lead to the words that come out of our mouths, which finally lead to the energies we emit out into the world. It's like a game of dominoes. The time it takes for a thought to trigger the emotion which triggers the energy which triggers the string of verbal or physical responses is lightning fast. Once it starts, there's no stopping it. But if you practice paying attention to the process, and you slow down just enough to hop off the turmoil train (if it's indeed about to fall off the rails), you're affecting change in a deep and powerful way.

I believe that most of us know when we're giving out good vibes and when we're not. My rule of thumb: If I wouldn't want to be on the receiving end of what I'm saying, how I'm behaving, or the energy that's emanating from me, then I need to stop, recalibrate, and find a better way. But guess what? Lucky for you, the rest of this chapter is a whole bunch of better ways! So you don't even have to find them anymore! Now, you just have to learn them.

LET ME HEAR THAT FEEDBACK

Getting feedback (sometimes even unsolicited feedback) from the people we care about most can be a helpful start. Case in point: on more than one occasion, my son has told me that I can be a nag (clearly it's on more than one occasion, otherwise I wouldn't be a nag!). As I've mentioned, it's important to trust your own gut and listen to your own voice, but that doesn't mean you do so at the expense of the important relationships in your life. If my son has expressed something to me multiple times, then maybe he's seeing something I don't. So that forces me to ask myself, what vibe am I putting out that's causing me to be labeled a nag? I gave it some thought and asked myself "Maybe I *am* a nag." And sure enough, after some serious introspection, I was able to see how he could feel that way. Upon further meditation and looking into my thought patterns, I was able to hone in on the problem: my lack of trust. I'm asking my son to do something, but I don't trust that it's going to get done. That was my vibe. And he totally picked up on it (that smart little bastard)!

Here's how it would go down:

> 8:00am: "Hey babe, don't forget tonight is garbage night."
>
> My son: I know (*grunts*).
>
> 5:30pm (not done yet): "When are you going to take out the garbage?"
>
> My son: (*rolls his eyes*).
>
> 8:15pm (house still stinks): "Could you take out the garbage? Not sure why I have to ask so many times!"
>
> My son: (*walks away*).
>
> 11:00pm (nope, not yet!): "Are you freakin' kidding me? Take it out already!"

So damn frustrating! But I had to take responsibility. I could have handled it in a variety of different ways, but I chose the "repeat, three-peat, and four-peat" method, followed by threatening to take his allowance away, and taking the untouched garbage and putting it in his bed. (Yes, yes, I did. He really loved that one). The truth is I was thinking out of anger, which made him completely immune to the sound of my voice. In turn, the issue became less about the actual garbage and more about our mother-son relationship. He genuinely started to feel that I cared more about garbage than I cared about him. That was the turning point for me. That's when I decided to look inward and really check my vibe, my intention, and my approach. I sat with it for a few days, and one morning as I was meditating, I had an 'a-ha' moment: *If my son has a bad taste in his mouth from my seemingly nagging demands, maybe someone else should be doing the demanding.* I tested my theory, and asked my husband to be in charge of overseeing garbage duties. Worked like a charm!

If you've tried changing someone else over and over again and the situation stays the same, that's a clue that you're working on the wrong person.

I'm imagining at this moment you might be feeling like I'm letting my son off the hook. "Sheira, you're an idiot. You're the mom. You're in charge. Your son is being ungrateful, irresponsible, and lazy. Lay down the law!" That's a very logical and warranted reaction to this scenario. However, take a moment to think about areas in your life, specifically relationships, that don't seem to be working as well as you'd like. One definition of "insanity" is doing the same thing over and over again and expecting a different result. Sometimes, although we don't agree with the people in our lives, it's up to us to make the move that breaks the cycle of insanity. It comes down to a choice between acting entirely stubborn and being *right*, or making a few concessions and being *happy*. Waiting for the other person to change is like waiting for a train in the middle of the desert. It ain't comin'! And the more you insist they change instead of looking inside for an alternative solution or approach, the more miserable and frustrated you'll be. Inside-out folks, inside-out!

LEAVE ME ALONE-UH!

Let's use another example. This time, strictly mother-daughter related. Moms, say your daughter comes home from school and she's clearly upset. You ask her how her day was. She unconvincingly says, "Fine." You have two eyes so you are able to see that it absolutely was not fine, and you want to know more. You delve a little deeper: "Honey, you seem upset. Tell me what happened." She doesn't want to. You ask her if she wants a snack. She says "no" but it sounds more like a bark. You say, "Hey, don't take your anger out on me! I didn't do anything to you." She gets up and goes to her room in a huff and under her breath says, "Just leave me alone!" You get annoyed because you're being a caring mom and she's being a… (well, I'll let you fill in the blank).

It's not uncommon, or even unreasonable, for you to feel that way about your daughter in those instances. But what you may not see is that you're taking things personally without being aware of what's really going on. Plus, you're allowing her yucky vibe to impact yours. Of course you want to help! That's the motherly instinct at work We want to help, fix, analyze, discuss, and advise. But here's the kicker. At that moment, *that may not be what your daughter needs from you*. Sometimes, if we really want to be helpful, we need to read the vibe, see that it's low on the spectrum, make a conscious decision not to get sucked in, and simply ask ourselves how we can be most helpful in that moment.

So now, let's rewind…

Your daughter comes home from school and she's clearly upset. You ask her how her day was. She unconvincingly says, "Fine." You have two eyes, so you are able to see that it absolutely was not fine... but instead of feeling the immediate need to interrogate, you say, "Hey, I can see you're not in a good place. If you want to talk, I'm here. If not, that's OK, too." By observing and making a choice to not get emotionally invested right away, you're saving yourself — and her — from potential heartache and unnecessary fighting.

It's not easy to keep your positive vibe when surrounded by negative ones. It takes strength, courage, consistency, determination, and perspective. But I promise, you have all of them inside of you. The more you can meet someone's negative vibe with compassion, empathy, and some level of detachment the more peaceful your home will be. Inevitably, there will be times when you'll be brought down by other people's energy; we're humans, not robots. But now that you have that awareness, you can work on influencing and lifting others with *your* energy to kick start a cycle of better vibes!

WHAT IS IT ABOUT BABIES AND PUPPIES?

"Unadulterated" means pure, untainted, or untouched. Is it just a coincidence that the word "adult" is in there? I think not! Perhaps our younger selves are unadulterated versions of the adults we grow up to be. I've always believed that children are wise beyond their years and have much to teach us. I'm constantly in awe of their presence, curiosity, resilience, honesty, and acceptance of all people. They're like little magnets for my heart. I love being around them!

It's the same with puppies (all dogs... but especially puppies). They give out such incredible energy. That's why we love being around them. Like babies, they exude a sense of joy and unconditional love to which adults can only aspire. Why do you think only dogs can respond to very high frequencies? Because that's where they live! (Vibe jokes! Yeah!)

I'm now going to present a series of photos comprised strictly of babies and puppies. As you look at each one, try to think of an adjective that describes the energy or vibe that the photo exudes.

Brace yourself, they're *really* cute!

What were some of the adjectives that came to mind? Adorable, sweet, innocent, curious, playful, happy? How did seeing those images affect you personally? I'm imagining that just looking at them for a second caused a positive shift in your vibe, even if it was only a slight one.

Babies and puppies are here to remind us of the joyful, sweet, wondrous living beings we all were... and still are. Re-engage with and nurture that part of yourself every day.

We are each born as a loving, kind, accepting, and compassionate soul. Somehow as we get older we lose some of these traits. It both fascinates and saddens me to see that, as we grow up, many of us become bitter, skeptical, unkind, and mistrusting. What happens to us, you ask? Life happens. We expand our horizons. We have more experiences in the world, and some of those experiences are frustrating, destructive, and downright horrifying. We start to judge. We start to fear. We start to see others as separate from ourselves. We compare. Our egos take over. And eventually, all these things pile up in our psyche causing us to look differently not only at others, but at ourselves as well.

The truth is we never actually lose those beautiful qualities we had as children. They just get buried. And, if we're going to be honest with ourselves, it's *we* who, on an unconscious level, allow this to happen. We allow — without realizing it — the consequences of the external world to squelch the magical qualities we had when we were younger (and for many of us, happier) selves. Being older, knowing more, and doing more, doesn't mean we have to become harsher or less trusting. It's our choice. If we're truly living from the inside-out, we can experience the negative things, people, and circumstances in the world and still choose to be loving, kind, accepting, and compassionate like the children we once were.

Here's an idea. Keep a photo of a favorite pet or a favorite kid (could be yourself as a child!) where you can see it every day. Focus on the vibe that that image is sending to you. Allow the image to be a reminder and guide of who you really are and who you want to be in this world.

SAY YES TO THE STRESS

This "Emotional Guidance Scale" from Abraham and Esther Hicks' book, *Ask And It Is Given* identifies the wide spectrum of the emotions we feel on a day-to-day basis:

1. Joy/appreciation/empowerment/freedom/love
2. Passion
3. Enthusiasm/eagerness/happiness
4. Positive expectation/belief
5. Optimism
6. Hopefulness
7. Contentment
8. Boredom
9. Pessimism
10. Frustration/irritation/impatience
11. Overwhelm
12. Disappointment
13. Doubt
14. Worry
15. Blame
16. Discouragement
17. Anger
18. Revenge
19. Hatred/rage
20. Jealousy

21. Insecurity/guilt/unworthiness

22. Fear/grief/depression/powerlessness

Notice how only the first seven emotions have positive connotations. That means the other 15 — which make up nearly 70% of this list — connote negativity. This means just what you think it means. It's easier to get sucked into the world of emotional despair as opposed to positive feelings. Often our first reaction to negative thoughts or feelings is to try and suppress or avoid them. But sometimes the only true way out is *through*. If you're in a bad place, the worry or jealousy or grief you're experiencing should be acknowledged, honored, and fully experienced. When you try to deny what you're feeling and put all your energy into trying to reverse or resist the pain, it'll only become worse. It's essential to *be* with whatever you're feeling. Some psychologists recommend that you actually label your emotion, connect with it, feel it deeply, write it down (even if you're crying and snotting in the process), and then make a decision to release it. If you're bold enough, take the piece of paper you wrote on and burn it (with proper fire safety precautions in place, of course). To fight against your emotions is to fight against yourself, and it's not a winning battle. When you're going through something difficult, you need to be on your own side. Support yourself. Let yourself feel. And then gradually, at your own pace (it could be weeks, months, or even years) let it go.

While being with and owning your emotions is extremely important, there are actions you can take to slowly shift your vibe when you're ready.

SOUNDS GOOD

Over the years I've asked teen girls what their most prevalent coping mechanism is. Their answer: listening to music. We all know intuitively that music has the power to change our vibrational frequency. When we're down and we hear something pleasant we often perk up almost immediately. Science knows it too. Dr. Masaru Emoto (weird that his last name is "Emoto" which sounds like "emotion") conducted this crazy, cool experiment to prove that sound waves (specifically musical waves) alter the chemical makeup of water crystals.

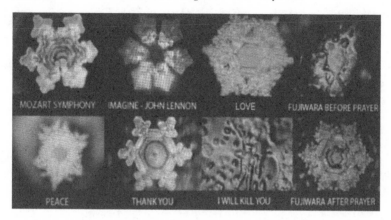

Look at the water crystals that are exposed to energy that is in alignment with the attributes we cherish (love, peace, gratitude, etc.). They're beautiful! But then, look at the ones exposed to the destructive, violent energy of hatred. It's all scattered and mixed up. The "water memory" present in his findings shows that emotional intention can dramatically shape the way water crystallizes. Dr. Emoto's work exemplifies how not only music, but also our inner thoughts and emotions have the power to alter our physical states. When you understand the impact of energy, it can help you reframe everything!

SMILE THOUGH YOUR HEART IS ACHING

Another helpful skill to practice (weird as it might seem) is smiling. Yup, the simple act of raising both ends of your mouth does wonders to improve your vibe. The first time I gave it a try, I was shocked to see how effective it was.

One time, when my daughter was about 14 years old, we were having a chat and she made a self-loathing comment about the way she looked. Unfortunately, I didn't fully hear what she said since she was speaking "teen" at 85 miles an hour, so I responded in a rushed way. She then somehow took my response to mean I agreed with her self-deprecating comment, which in turn sent her into a full-on meltdown. From then on, everything I said was construed as "yelling at her." Yet, in my mind, I couldn't have been more compassionate or understanding.

"Stop yelling at me!" she screamed again and again as she stomped up the stairs. She slammed the door to her bedroom so hard I thought the entire house would collapse. That was my trigger point. Enraged by the slamming, and exhausted from trying to defend myself, I hurled back a series of obnoxious retorts through my gritted teeth (Couldn't let her have the last word, now could I?) and ran into the bathroom to escape. But suddenly, I caught a glimpse of myself in the mirror and felt my entire body jolt. The face staring back at me was beyond scary (think Wicked Witch from *The Wizard of Oz* meets Ursula from *The Little Mermaid*). I gaped in horror at my reflection all the while thinking, "Holy cow, is this what I look like when I'm angry?" It was quite an eye opening experience (although I wanted to shut them immediately).

In an attempt to erase the frightening face in the mirror, I took 10 deep breaths. My blood pressure started descending from Mount Everest, and suddenly I remembered the smiling technique. And so very begrudgingly, but very intentionally, I forced a smile. Right on cue, I felt my body energy start to shift. After a few minutes, I was in such a different head that I was able to make better decisions from a healthier place. Plus, knowing that I made that shift happen *on my own* was empowering. The conversation with my daughter that followed came from a more empathic place, and we were able to smooth things over.

Moral of the story: Smiles make the world go 'round.

I AM SUPERWOMAN

Another very interesting vibe-enriching technique I came across in my research is called "Power Posing." Harvard University Professor Amy Cuddy did extensive research on what our body language reveals about not only how others perceive us but how we perceive ourselves. Her research shows that people in leadership or influential positions (for example, CEOs, celebrities, government leaders, etc.) tend to naturally pose authoritatively, while those who feel insecure or unworthy tend to pose unassumingly. She concluded that our body language informs our minds, which then influences our words and, subsequently, our behavior.

For some people, power posing comes naturally. For others, it takes a bit more effort to feel comfortable holding your body in such a way. But don't be intimidated. A little power posing can go a long way. Trying out a power pose — even for just a minute or two on a consistent basis — positively influences self-perception.

Evidently, our body language and our vibe go hand in hand. For many girls and women, our inclination is to make ourselves physically unobtrusive and inconspicuous. But what that does from a vibe perspective is make us feel like we're unimportant. Think about that for a second. We so often blame society, the media, or men for making us feel insignificant. This study shows that we are also doing the very same to *ourselves*.

As I mentioned at the very beginning, women's contributions are vital to the balance of the world. We possess many strengths of which we should be proud. Instead of hiding from the world by shrinking ourselves (both physically and mentally), we need to stand up proudly and face the world knowing that we have something unparalleled to offer. We are important. We matter.

Internalize, ponder, and digest that for a minute Superwoman!

LISTEN TO ALBERT

According to Albert Einstein, one of the most important questions we can ask every day is "Do I believe I'm living in a friendly or a hostile world?" The answer to that question determines the kind of vibe we give off throughout the day. If every one of us decided that the universe is indeed friendly, cooperative, and loving imagine the collective impact that could have. Deliberating Albert Einstein's question is the first step. Following through on the answer is another.

Make a conscious decision to put the right energy out into the world. It will help you sleep better at night. It will help you maintain your health. It will help you grow as a person. When you consistently emit good vibes, even when others don't, you are living life in the best possible way: from the inside-out.

Key VIBE takeaways:

- You are more than just skin, bones, hair and teeth! You are a miraculous, dynamic field of energy.

- Be aware of the vibration and energy you're giving off at all times. If you wouldn't want to be on the receiving end of it, change it. You're in charge!

- Try power posing, smiling, or listening to your favorite tunes when you're feeling down. Practicing any of these will shift your energy, vibe, and perspective.

A_ _ _ _ _ _ _

I reap what I sow

T here is a word in the English language that, when you add up the numerical value of each of its letter (A=1; B=2; C=3; and so on), equals exactly 100.

That word is: ATTITUDE.

A =	1
T =	20
T =	20
I =	9
T =	20
U =	21
D =	4
E =	5
TOTAL =	**100**

My dad always told me that attitude is everything. Looks like he was right.

Your attitude is the way you view the world. It's your mindset, your perspective, your outlook. Having a "positive attitude" means seeing life as a glass half full, whereas having a "negative attitude" means seeing life as an old cracked mug with three-week old coffee stains on the bottom. We've already talked a great deal about the power of positivity. So in this chapter, the alternative definition of attitude — a resentful or antagonistic way of communicating — is the one we'll focus on.

IT'S NOT WHAT YOU SAY, IT'S HOW YOU SAY IT

In school, we teach children many subjects. Critical among them is English. We teach spelling, comprehension, writing, punctuation, grammar, and syntax. We teach them all the words they'll ever need to know. But we don't always teach them how to *use* those words effectively. Our speech and intonation are just as important as our language. They make an enormous difference in the way thoughts are relayed, so they affect the outcome of the conversation in which they are used. When we become aware of not only what we say but how we say it, we open ourselves up to a whole new level of empowerment.

Knowing the right things to say is useless if you don't know the right ways to say them.

Stop and think for a second about the fact that you can speak. You are manipulating your lips, tongue, vocal cords, and breath to push sound out that ultimately relays thoughts and feelings to another human being. It's a miracle that unfortunately most of us take for granted. To think that we have this incredible ability, and we're squandering it on negativity, is just plain upsetting. With every judgmental, impatient, derogatory, and unnecessarily harsh word we say, we throw away our potential to affect positive change. On the contrary, by using our words to lift others up, show appreciation, express love, and peacefully resolve conflict we gain the facility to make enormous differences, not just in our own lives but in the lives of those around us. To paraphrase from practically every movie ever made, we need to use our powers for good and not evil!

CHANGE THE CHANNEL

As moms we tend to inherit the good, the bad, and the ugly from the way our parents spoke to us, and unconsciously pass it onto our children. Many of us vow never to be like our parents only to start saying the very things we resented in our youth. It's like a rerun of a bad soap opera!

What's going on here is simply a lack of awareness. When we don't pay attention to the words we say or how we say them, we're just knee-jerk reacting to everything. Contrary to what the famous "sticks and stones" poem implies, words really can hurt. A lot. Especially for us females. We tend to be quite sensitive and over-analytical — not to mention, we remember *everything*! As a result, we often turn into Wolverine when we are wronged, hurling harsh words like blades at whoever dares to insult us.

Using mean, harsh words is a form of abuse.
If you want to break that cycle, you need to
change not only the words you choose,
but your intonation as well.

Once a word comes out of your mouth, however, you are no longer the master, you are the slave. How many times can you remember regretting saying something the second it came out of your mouth? You may beg for forgiveness from whomever you verbally injured...

but sometimes it's too late. The words have already done irreparable damage.

Yelling, blaming, punishing, shaming — those things are easy to do. But it's harder, and therefore more rewarding, to speak calmly, understand, empathize, and praise. And while none of those actions may seem totally natural in a stressful moment, you'd be shocked at how effective they can be. You don't have to do what you've always done. If negativity doesn't serve you — and let's face it, it never truly has — there has to be a better way. When it comes to language, replacing even one negative word with a more positive one can lead you down a different path. It's time to change the channel; the boring old soap opera isn't your only choice anymore.

COMMUNICATING WITH COMPASSION

Now that we've established all the trouble our negativity-fueled communication can get us into, how do we stop? There's a little known language communication platform developed by a man named Marshall Rosenberg back in the 1960s called Non-Violent Communication (NVC). It emphasizes compassion as the motivation for action, rather than fear, guilt, shame, blame, coercion, threat, or punishment.

NVC's premise is that all human beings have universal needs. We all have a need to be heard, included, respected, loved, appreciated, and cherished. When we're in touch with what we fundamentally need in any given moment, we approach others and ourselves from a place of awareness, as opposed to confusion or frustration. To clarify, NVC is *not* about getting people to be or do what you want and nothing else. It's about creating a core quality of connection that meets *everyone's* needs. If we can begin to relate to ourselves and others from a place of meeting needs then there's no room for the negative stuff.

So how does it work? NVC's work is based on the acronym OFNR, which stands for Observation, Feeling, Need, and Request. Below is a basic outline of this platform, followed up with some tangible examples. I strongly suggest to moms and daughters that you visit the NVC website (www.cnvc.org) to learn more… and possibly even take a course together! Their motto is "connection *before* correction." Keep that in mind as you read the rest of this chapter.

OBSERVATION

Most of us are totally asleep at the wheel when we communicate. And since there's no mental traffic light telling us when to stop, go, or slow down we're often clueless as to what will help us most in any given moment. When you feel things going south it's always best to take a step back and assess the situation — to "proceed with caution." For example, if your daughter has copped a serious 'tude and is now angrily spewing at you, literally watch the words come out of her mouth, one by one. Consider attaching a color or a pattern to the words. Visualize black rocks coming out from between her lips. Or, observe the words as musical notes (maybe heavy metal)! Just notice. Don't instantly take it personally like you usually do. Listen and observe. Don't *say* anything!

FEELING

Once you have observed, notice the feelings that are stirring in you. At this point, you're likely feeling hurt, sad, or disappointed.

In your mind, label the feeling with the following template: *When I am spoken to this way, I feel [blank]*. It's important to speak in terms of "I" and not "you" when addressing your daughter (or mom), because using "you" places all the blame on her. When expressing your needs, it's much more effective to put the focus on *yourself*, and what is happening for *you*. NVC provides a list of identifiable emotions with which you can familiarize yourself. (And no, "my daughter's being a gigantic prima donna" is not on the list.) When you're tempted to say things like that, stop, let yourself feel, and adjust your language accordingly.

NEED

The practice of connecting with what you feel at any given moment will lead you to get in touch with what you need. When you can identify which of your needs is not being met, you can learn what it is that you value. For instance, if your daughter's tone and language are causing you to feel hurt, it becomes evident how much you value kindness and respect.

Earlier, I introduced a short list of needs; the NVC website offers a much more comprehensive one. When you read that list of needs, pay close attention, and see which ones resonate most with you and your experiences. Once you understand your needs as non-negotiables in your life, you will be that much better equipped to express them in an effective way.

REQUEST

The last step is the most important, and the most challenging. We must keep in mind that there's a vast difference between a *request* and a *demand.* Most of us want what we want when we want it, and can give off "demand" energy without even realizing it. But think about it — if you were on the receiving end of that kind of energy, you wouldn't be so willing to comply. On the contrary, when we emit "request" energy instead of "demand," the protons, electrons, and neutrons emanating from our body are more like a ballet and less like a body slam. The next time you're communicating, try and be conscious of whether you're requesting or demanding. The best way to remember which is which is knowing that a request is usually in the form of a question ("Would you be willing to…?" or "Are you open to…?"). And remember that when making a request, you need to be willing to accept a "No" from the other party.

As you practice these steps, you may very well be inclined to revert back to old behavior. Don't! Stay strong! Hold your tongue! You're trying something new, so it's going to feel unnatural in the beginning.

Any unfamiliar skill that you start practicing, no matter what it is (learning a new instrument, playing a sport, speaking a new language, etc.), is going to feel out of your comfort zone at first. Patience and persistence are the only things separating the successful from the unsuccessful. Don't give up.

COMPASSIONATE COMMUNICATION IN ACTION

Let's put this innovative communication platform in a real-world context. The following are two examples of common mother-daughter miscommunications. One is presented from the mom's perspective, and one from the daughter's — shown in both pre- and post-NVC versions.

Example #1:

You're a mom whose daughter refuses to clean her room. It looks like a hurricane hit a flea market in there. You've asked her to tidy up a million times, to no avail. Finally, you just can't take it anymore. This is the last straw.

> Mom: Ashley, your room looks like a bomb hit it! How many times have I asked you to clean it? Do it NOW!
>
> Ashley: Oh my G-d! Why do you come in here and start yelling at me? Can't you see I'm doing my homework? I'll do it when I get to it. Geez!!!!!
>
> Mom: I'm fed up with the way you treat your things! Clean it up now or you're grounded for a week!
>
> Ashley: STOP IT, MOM! I have a big test tomorrow!
>
> Mom: Okay, then you're grounded!
>
> Ashley: Get out of my room! I hate you!!!!!
>
> Aaaand… scene.

That's the kind of unconscious communication that many of us partic-
ipate in on a regular basis. Does it work? No. Do we keep doing it?
Yes. Why? Nobody knows. But here's what the same exact scenario
could sound like using Compassionate Communication:

> Mom: I notice that you have a lot of clothes on the floor.
> When I see how messy your room is, I feel frustrated because I
> value cleanliness and appreciation of the things we spend our
> hard-earned money on. Would you be willing to clean it up af-
> ter dinner tonight?
>
> Ashley: Who are you and what have you done with my mother?
>
> Aaaand… scene.

In the latter example, Mom is able to detach, observe, express what she
is feeling/needing, and end by calmly requesting her daughter's help to
correct the situation. By addressing each of these four steps, blame,
shame, and judgment are removed from the equation, making room for
a much healthier, more productive exchange.

Example #2:

You're a daughter who nonchalantly mentions her weekend plans to
her mom — only to be met with unexpected judgment.

> Jessica: I'm getting together with Lauren on Sunday.
>
> Mom: Lauren? Really? She hardly ever invites you anywhere;
> you're always inviting her.
>
> Jessica: What are you talking about? She's my friend!
>
> Mom: Friendship should be a two-way street!
>
> Jessica: Stop telling me who to be friends with! Who do you
> think you are?
>
> Mom: I'm your mom, that's who!

Jessica: Then act like one!!!!

Aaaand… scene.

When we speak with only our own perspective in mind, we're unable to assess the big picture. Ego-driven communication is dangerous! With a slight shift in tone, and a bit more emphasis placed on the words we choose, that very same conversation could have gone like this:

Jessica: I'm getting together with Lauren on Sunday.

Mom: Lauren? Really? She hardly ever invites you anywhere. You're always inviting her.

Jessica: Mom, when you question who I'm hanging out with, I feel angry. I wish you trusted me more to make my own decisions. How about I figure things out for myself and I'll come to you if I need advice… okay?

Mom: Here's a million dollars.

Aaaand… scene.

In this instance, Jessica is able to take a deep breath and catch herself before she goes down the rabbit hole. In doing so she gives herself space to detach, observe, express what she is feeling/needing, and end by calmly requesting her mom's understanding.

I want to recognize that these scenarios tend to oversimplify things. Life is not a half-hour sitcom where things get resolved between commercial breaks; it's more complicated than that.

But it doesn't have to be. If you make a conscious decision to change what you say and the way you say it, the results can be tremendous. You might not totally recognize yourself in the NVC versions of the exchanges above… but that's kind of the point. Change often means giving something totally foreign a fighting chance. Just remember NVC's pneumonic device: *connection before correction.* Try it and you'll see for yourself. You have nothing to lose except your bad attitude!

THE PERSPECTIVE PILL

Another way to temper your attitude is to take a drug. It's not the kind of drug your health teacher has warned you about; it's called "The Perspective Pill."

In his book *The 7 Habits of Highly Effective People*, bestselling author Steven Covey shares a story about a man who gets onto a subway with his three small children. The kids run rampant through the car, screaming and acting out as the other passengers try to read their newspapers, or talk to their friends. The father just sits there, looking down, ignoring his children completely. One passengers becomes so irritated that she marches right up to the father and says, in a harsh tone: "You know, you should really do something about your kids." The father slowly lifts his head up and says, "I'm so sorry. We just came from the hospital. Their mother died about an hour ago. I don't know how to tell them."

You truly never know what other people are going through in their lives — but when you witness firsthand the difficulties people face, it can cause a significant attitude adjustment.

The difficulty in question doesn't necessarily need to be as severe as losing a spouse to warrant empathy. In the day-to-day case of women and girls, the issue might be a fight with a relative, a bad illness, or romance on the rocks. If you were experiencing something that wounded your well-being, you'd want your friends and family to be understanding. You should be understanding too. Remember what I said earlier. Attitudes can do a lot of damage in very little time. There's no need to risk your relationships with your loved ones by being careless about the way you communicate. It's never worth it.

Make sure to take a perspective pill every day.
Eventually it'll go down easy!

The Perspective Pill can also be used to shift your tainted perception of your own life. We all experience varying degrees of hardship through-out our lives — but chances are, at any given moment, your problems will pale in comparison to someone else's problems. I fully understand that this kind of reasoning won't necessarily resonate with teenage girls (for example, knowing that kids are starving in Africa will not always make our children eat their veggies). However, moms shouldn't stop bringing those discrepancies to their daughters' attention. They just need to do so in a more direct, innovative way. A few suggestions:

1. *The Interwebs.* Sharing videos, images, and stories of people experiencing serious challenges (physical, mental, cultural, economic) - whether it's in third world countries or in your own neighborhood - can be extremely thought-provoking, especially when accompanied by a conversation.

2. *Personal Histories.* Openly discussing the struggles you (or those close to you) have faced can make a true impact on a child's heart and mind. I shared with you some of my father's story, but my mother has also endured hardship and tragedy that have shaped my sense of perspective (more on that in the next chapter).

3. *Charity Work.* Bring your family to volunteer in your community. When my kids were young, my husband and I made a habit of volunteering as a family at a local food pantry. We would fill up the car and make several rounds of drop-offs to families in need. We didn't just drop off the food. We took the time to talk with these people and hear their stories. Interacting with fellow human beings from other walks of life

incurs a heightened appreciation for all that we have —
something we could certainly use a bit more of these days.

GET 'EM WHILE THEY'RE YOUNG

A few years ago I was commissioned by a school to write a theme song
about the power of words that aligned with the school's new motto
"Smart Choices, Kind Voices." The school recognized the importance
and strength of words and teaching this critical skill when kids are
young — when their minds are still fertile ground for new suggestions,
modes, and ways of thinking. At the end of the poem are three lines
that I believe sum up the importance of doing away with attitudes, and
any form of mal-intentioned communication:

Words have started wars
Words have opened doors
How will you use yours?

Key ATTITUDE takeaways:

- Words are more powerful than we can imagine. Be mindful of the ones you choose, and more importantly, how you use them. If you wouldn't be okay being on the receiving end of what you're about to say, think twice about saying it.

- Before spouting at the mouth, take a moment to consider what fundamental need isn't being met, and choose to phrase your words in the context of that need.

- Attitude affects action, action affects outcome.

THANKFULNESS

Let my gratitude show

M y relationship with my mother has always been — for lack of a better word — interesting. Looking back on my childhood, I remember my mother as very nurturing, loving, and doting. When I transitioned into adolescence, however, her attitude toward me seemed to change overnight; I felt her unconditional love quickly and inexplicably turn to jealousy and resentment. To make matters worse, our enormous culture gap distanced us even further. My mom moved to America from Israel only a year before I was born, so she didn't know the first thing about what was "cool" or "in" and I often ended up feeling embarrassed by her lack of social awareness. The cherry atop this nightmare sundae was her volatile relationship with my dad; they fought incessantly as a result of their troubled marriage, and I escaped to be with friends as often as I could.

In adulthood, the conflict with my mom only intensified. Shortly after I graduated from college, I met the man who would eventually become my husband. My mom immediately disapproved of him and she made no bones about it. Over the next five years, things between my mother and me were at an all-time low. I couldn't even look her in the eye when talking to her. At times, I wasn't sure our relationship could even be salvaged.

When I was in my 30's, I started on a personal development journey and a friend recommended a book called *Loving What Is* by Byron Katie. The book's premise is based on an exercise called "The Work," in which you attempt to remedy an issue that perpetually plagues you. First, you identify the issue — more specifically, a challenging person or circumstance in your life. Next, you summarize your main point of contention with that person or circumstance into one clear statement. Then, Katie presents four questions to ask yourself regarding said statement with the goal of altering your outlook.

I'm sure it won't surprise you to hear that I chose my relationship with my mother as the "issue." After some deliberation, I settled on a one-line point of contention: "My mother should listen to me and understand me more." And then, it was question time.

1. Is it true? (Yes or No)

It was a no-brainer — YES! My mother should *absolutely* listen to me and understand me more. I'm her daughter! She should want to know how I feel and take the time to comprehend why. That's all part of the mother gig!

2. Can you absolutely know that it's true? (Yes or No)

Again, affirmative! The woman who gave me life is barely invested in my emotional well-being. How is that fair? I — like everyone else — am deserving of that care and attention.

3. How do you react — what happens — when you believe that thought?

When I believe the thought that my mother should listen to me and understand me more, I become incredibly frustrated... because she doesn't. It was at this point that I started to see how believing the thought that my mother should listen to and understand me more brings me the opposite of what I want, which is peace.

4. Who would you be without the thought?

I paused here, and sat quietly with this final question for a long time. I visualized what I would be like if I was with my mother and simply didn't believe the thought that she should listen to me and understand me more. I supposed I would be... happier? Free? In control? Now things were getting interesting...

The final step of "The Work" is something called "The Turnaround," in which you must turn the statement around three times — to yourself, to the other person, and to the opposite statement. In my case, "My mother should listen to and understand me more" turns around to:

- I should listen to and understand myself more.

- I should listen to and understand my mother more.

- My mother shouldn't listen to me and understand me more.

It was then that I experienced a major breakthrough — another tomahawk moment. After years of lugging around resentment towards her for not being the mother I wanted, it dawned on me that I need to be looking at her not so much as my mother, but more so as my teacher — my teacher of what *not* to do. My mother has taught me many positive things in my life: honesty, sensitivity, a love of music, the importance of heritage, and more. But the negative things — including the behavior she was modeling that I did not value — were *also* teaching me extremely valuable lessons — self-awareness, and perhaps more importantly, compassion. Once I stopped brushing aside the truth about the reason my mother is the way she is, I was able to understand what I should have all along.

The truth is my mother had a very painful upbringing. She grew up poor and emotionally abused at the hands of *her* mother, who would lock her clothes in a closet so she couldn't go out with boys. She force-fed her. She told her she was "no good" and "worthless" on a daily basis. She was grossly mistreated, on all accounts, and it did irreparable damage. So no wonder she couldn't be the kind of mother I wanted — she didn't know *how*. She was never given the chance! But guess what? *I was.* I was given the chance. All I needed to do was break the cycle, and do things differently. So thank you Mom, for being my teacher.

"The Work," when done with an open mind and heart, shows us that much of our internal suffering is brought on by the belief of our own thoughts. When I was able to say the words "thank you for teaching me what *not* to do" — and actually believe them — I felt a surge of gratitude. I always understood the importance of being thankful, but the idea that I could be grateful for the *crappy* things in my life? That was a new concept for me. However, not only did I feel gratitude in that moment, but something else emerged as well: compassion. I felt a deep sadness for her and everything she went through. At that moment, I wished that I could literally take a ladle and scoop some of my awareness into her soul, like homemade chicken soup. When you're able to accept all that is happening around you (good and bad) as an inevitable lesson of sorts, you begin to look at your life with fresh eyes.

Malachy McCourt said: "Resentment is like drinking poison expecting the other person to die."

Thinking back on how severely I'd poisoned myself for so many years before coming to that realization about my mother, I couldn't help but think what a waste it was. All the anger, frustration, the screaming and yelling, the brick walls I came up against over and over… it suddenly didn't seem worth it. "What an incredible waste of time trying to change her," I thought to myself. But the more I thought about it, the more I realized it was those obstacles that led me to that moment of incredible awareness. At the end of the day, time we spend learning — no matter how long, arduous, or exhausting — is never time wasted.

DANKE SCHOEN

Manners are something we learn very early on in life. Phrases such as "please," "you're welcome," "excuse me," and of course, thank you," are often some of the first in our vocabulary. But these phrases shouldn't be used exclusively for the purpose of respecting others; these phrases should also be used for the purpose of respecting *ourselves*. By acknowledging how fortunate we are to have certain people and things in our lives, we fill up a part of our consciousness that makes it harder for negativity to strong-arm its way in. As we discussed in Chapter 2, your mind cannot process two thoughts at the exact same time. If you choose the positive thought, there's simply no room for the negative one. In this vein, it's impossible to be grateful and bitter at the same time. So why not choose gratitude?

HOW MUCH DO YOU REALLY NEED, ANYWAY?

A very wise (and anonymous) person once said, "The richest person is not the one who has the most, but the one who needs the least." In our overly materialistic society, we'd all do ourselves a favor (spiritually, emotionally, and certainly financially) to embrace this quote. When you think about it, life is transient and temporary. We don't really own things. We just use them while we're here. When we're gone, they're not ours anymore.

Tom Shadyac has directed some of the world's biggest blockbuster movies including *Liar Liar*, *Bruce Almighty*, and *The Nutty Professor*. Unfortunately, all his fame and success didn't prevent tragedy from striking. A devastating biking accident in 2007 left him with a severe case of post-concussion syndrome. This resulted in perpetual suffering from acute headaches and light sensitivity. After eight months of unbearable pain, he prayed for death. But as fate would have it, one day, he woke up completely healed. He stood at the top of the stairs of his 17,000 square foot mansion, complete with chef, driver, groundskeeper, butler, and maid… and realized that he wasn't actually happy. Feeling like he'd been given a second chance, he decided to travel the world with a camera crew interviewing some of the world's top environmentalists, religious leaders, and spiritual gurus about the true source of people's happiness. The result was an inspiring documentary entitled *I Am*.

In one of the film' interviews, Shadyac concludes that if you have absolutely nothing (like my father, when he was hiding in the forest) and someone gives you a roof over your head, a bowl of soup, and some warm clothes, you experience a significant increase in your level of happiness. However, when you go from having all the basics to having a million dollars and a million luxuries, you don't become a million times happier.

Take a look around and tell me what we, as a society, are modeling for our children. What are we teaching them about happiness? We teach them if they do well in school, go to college, get a job, make money, and buy things, they'll be happy. We honestly believe — and the advertising world reinforces — that if we have lots of things we'll be complete. What they don't tell us is that we'll eventually break our backs from working too hard to keep up with our own delusional desires. It's a rat race where there are no winners. Only rats.

The moment you realize that having more things will not necessarily make you happier, you'll be happier.

Clothes, shoes, watches, jewelry, electronics… it's all the same. We buy them, we experience the brief spurt of joy that comes with each purchase, and we feel accomplished over having acquired a new possession. But a good portion of the time, that thing ends up tucked away in a drawer, box, or closet never to be seen again. Why? Because a few days later, there's a brand new item that catches our eye, and we set our sights on that instead. And the vicious cycle starts all over again.

The mighty media understand this psychological phenomenon all too well, and consequently target us with specially crafted messages and images to convince us of what we "have to" have. The more aware you are, the more evident it becomes that we are living in a giant marketing machine with the singular goal of making more coin! These strategic marketing ploys keep coming at us a hundred miles a minute for no other reason than *we let them*. We let them, we get sucked in… and before you know it their ridiculous campaigns actually work. They end up with lots of money, and we end up with lots of stuff we don't need.

Think about makeup commercials. Nine times out of ten, it goes a little something like this:

> Tall, thin, gorgeous model walks in slow motion down the street.

> Tall, thin, gorgeous model bats her eyelashes at some random dude.

> Tall, thin, gorgeous model becomes the object of random dude's desires.

Tall, thin, gorgeous model lives happily ever after.

Guess what? Tall, thin, gorgeous model just sold you mascara. Mascara that's made for $2 a tube and sold to gullible customers like you for $20 a tube. The best part? Tall, thin, gorgeous model is really normal, well-lit, airbrushed girl. You won't look like that when you use the mascara. Not even *she* looks like that when she uses the mascara. It's really astonishing what technology these days can do.

Alarming as it may be, our daughters deserve to know that it's huge corporations that are defining happiness for them — not to mention body image and self-worth. Once they know this, it will go without saying that these media conglomerates *do not* have their best interests at heart. Their only interest — heck, their only real job — is to *make money*! Money for the company, executives, and shareholders. It's that simple. The flawless footage of seemingly flawless girls that these companies propagate are there to touch your wallet, not your soul. They will go to extreme lengths to make their product, however frivolous, appear to be the most desirable thing on the whole planet. Retouching, custom lighting, special effects, an enormous team of professional makeup artists, hairstylists, and wardrobe personnel — these are the tools they have at their disposal. Remember, you would look über-glamorous too if you were made up by a personal styling team, sat in front of a giant fan, and then placed under perfect lighting that took three hours to set up. Our girls need to know that they're witnessing a world that *does not exist*. It reminds me of the end of *The Wizard of Oz*, where they pull back the curtain to reveal the wizard awkwardly trying to keep up the charade and cover up the fact that he's a total fraud. If we can dispel the perfection myth for our girls while they're still young, it will give them the impetus to further explore and question the world in which they live.

The bottom line is the following overused but ever-so-true phrase: money can't buy happiness. "Things" won't make us happy no matter how many of them we have. In fact, the insatiability of amassing "things" can actually cause a *decrease* in happiness and fulfillment because we imprudently rely on them to boost our spirits. We have been conditioned to believe that "things" are the key to joy, when in reality, the key is our loved ones and the experiences we share with them. We must begin to question the constant need for *more*. Right now, *more* means more clothes, more jewelry, more horsepower, more living space. But what this world really needs more of is kindness, tolerance, charity, and of course, thankfulness.

WORK FOR IT

I hear many adults today complaining that this generation of young adults has a disproportionate sense of entitlement. They act like the world owes them something, and they should be able to get whatever they want whenever they want. Shame on them! But wait just a pancake-flippin' second. Aren't adults the ones raising this generation? Don't we have to take responsibility for creating an environment that enables that mentality? If we don't want to raise a bunch of ungrateful spoiled brats, we need to stop giving them everything they want. We need to teach that if *they* want something, *they* need to be the ones to make it happen. Because when our children are taught to do chores from an early age, get a job when they come of age, and save their money, they start to learn what *enough* looks like. We're not doing our children any favors by serving them everything on a silver platter. Make your kids work for what they want — and model a solid work ethic, so they know firsthand how to do it.

If we give our children what they can provide for themselves, how will they ever learn to be self-sufficient?

As parents, we need to ask ourselves this fundamental question: why are we giving our children almost everything they ask for? There are several potential reasons we give in. Maybe we're subconsciously over-compensating for the lack we experienced in our own childhood. Maybe we're not around for our kids as much as we think we should be because we're working too much, and this is our guilty conscience's way of making it up to them. Maybe we're just trying to "keep up with the Joneses." (By the way, who are those damn Joneses? I want a phone number and address. I need to tell them to take it down a notch!) Whatever the reason is, we need to identify it so we can correct the problem. We don't need to give our kids too much because we didn't have enough. Buying them things will never be an equivalent for the quality time we're sacrificing. And showering our kids with lots of stuff simply to impress other people is an especially horrible example to be setting. If we're teaching our daughters to build their lives around what other people think, then it's no wonder all they say is, "I have to have those shoes, Mom — all the other girls are wearing them!" and "I can't believe we're not going on vacation this winter — everyone else is!" By spending more time keeping up appearances than instilling our children with the proper morals, we're creating the very problem which we so often complain about.

Model gratitude and appreciation often
and you will start to feel a shift in
your home and in your heart.

On the flip side, when our daughters see and hear us being grateful — for our health, food, home, friends, family, and for the experience of simply being alive — they incorporate a vital lesson into their soon-to-be adult worlds: *I have a lot to be grateful for, and it's all around me.*

Filling your home with expressions of gratitude and appreciation can immediately shift the vibe therein — and it's up to us moms to get the ball rolling. Out in the world, our daughters are constantly bombarded with academic pressure, nasty rumors, complaints, stress, and judgment. Our homes need to be sacred places where words of gratitude and appreciation are expressed freely and abundantly. When we say these things in front of our daughters, they listen: "Wasn't that a delicious meal?"... "Thank you for holding the door"... "We're very blessed to have our health." Don't worry if progress is slow. It's not likely that your daughter will immediately start spewing a bevy of thank-you's. Just trust that the example you set directly influences the kind of person she will become.

HAVE-TA VS. WANT-TA

When my daughter was little, she used to ask me for many things, as most little kids do: "Can we bake cookies?"... "Can we go see the new Disney movie?"... "Can we go to the mall tomorrow?" In many instances, it would be followed with "I *have* to have them!" or "I *have* to see it!" or "We *have* to go!" My husband and I made it a regular practice to look her right in the eye and ask, "Do you *have* to have it or do you *want* to have it?" This was known in our family as "have-ta, want-ta." I highly recommend calling your kids out on the things they claim they *have* to have. They must understand the difference between needing and wanting in order to begin prioritizing things for themselves. If we don't instill this value while they're still under our roofs, we're potentially setting them up not only for financial ruin, but for emotional deprivation. When they work hard for the things they desire, they inherently learn to separate necessities from luxuries — and they learn to be grateful to you for showing them the way.

Before you consider buying something
ask yourself: Do I *have* to have it or
do I *want* to have it?

Here's an interesting "have-ta, want-ta" exercise you can do with your daughter or on your own. Take a piece of paper divide it into four quadrants. Then, add a row at the top, and a column on the left. Then, write "Have" and "Don't Have" on the top, and "Want" and "Don't Want" on the left side. Then, fill it in, like so:

Each quadrant teaches its own lesson.

	HAVE	DON'T HAVE
WANT	– Home – Family – Health – Pet lizard named Jarvis	– Confidence – Expensive outfit – Clear skin – Cute barista from coffee shop
DON'T WANT	– Clumsiness – Messy bedroom – Frizzy hair – Perpetually angry boss	– Rare disease – Being homeless – Going to a funeral – Eating crickets for dinner

First, we have the "Have/Want" quadrant. When you look at this quadrant, it's the perfect opportunity to sit back and be truly grateful for the things you have and also want. Really ponder that for a minute: you have it *and* you want it. That's pretty damn awesome, if you ask me.

Next, the "Have/Don't Want" quadrant highlights the importance of acceptance. Simply being with *what is* is also a form of gratitude. You may not want the messy room or the frizzy hair or an obnoxious boss, but that's what's happening right now. If you can better a situation instead of complaining about it, do just that! If not, acceptance is often equally as helpful in terms of maintaining a peaceful state of mind.

As for the "Don't Have/Want" quadrant, these are things to be grateful for getting the chance to work toward. You can practice building confidence by getting the nerve to talk to that cute barista or save money for that gorgeous but expensive outfit. Be grateful, in advance, for the results that will come from your efforts.

Finally, the "Don't Have/Don't Want" quadrant reminds us to be grateful for things we *don't* have. There are millions of people in the world dealing with all kinds of health challenges, family issues, financial turmoil — even violence and war! Take a moment to be super grateful if you are not facing these kinds of crises in your life right now.

Gratitude comes in many shapes and sizes. Expand your definition of gratitude and your heart will thank you for it.

THANK YOU TO ME

When was the last time you said 'Thank you' to yourself?

Girls, you're all thinking to yourselves: "Huh?" And moms are saying one of two things:

(1) "*Me* say thank you to *myself*? Are you kidding? Everyone else should be saying thank you to me, but do they? No. It's the most thankless job in the world. And the pay stinks!"

OR

(2) "Who has time? I'm too busy running around like a chicken with my head cut off either working, playing chauffeur, running errands, breaking up my kids' fights, helping with homework,

cooking, cleaning, and doing laundry. I'm living in the movie *Groundhog's Day*. There's just no time for gratitude!"

To both of these arguments, I say, "I get it." But you know the phrase "We teach others how to treat us"? When we show ourselves gratitude we're showing those around us how we expect to be treated. We can certainly start by saying the actual words "Thank you" to ourselves for being the fabulous females that we are. Just try it out for a hot minute. Look at yourself and say, "Thank you for all your hard work. It's amazing what you get done in a day! You do so much for others… you're a good person, dammit!" It doesn't have to be those exact words, but you get the idea. It might feel unnatural and corny, but after a while, you'll begin to feel a shift in the way you view yourself and present yourself to the world. Progress takes time and change happens gradually. Don't give up. Why? Ask L'Oreal.[3]

> Living from the inside-out means being grateful for yourself first.

And, since actions speak louder than words, we should also be expressing gratitude to ourselves through self-care — whatever that means to you. Carve out a consistent time slot during the day or during the week that's *just for you* — to exercise, meditate, journal, volunteer, practice a hobby, take a bubble bath, go out with friends, read a book, or whatever floats your boat! When we're no good to ourselves, we're no good to anyone. We must re-charge our batteries on a regular basis. For example, let your family and friends know that Saturdays from 8:00am-10:00am is *me* time! Put up a sign if you need to! When you put your stake in the ground in committing to be grateful to *yourself*, you're also

---

[3] L'Oreal's tagline is "Because you're worth it." (Again, not a paid endorsement, just a relevant reference.)

doing double-duty by showing your daughter that you value yourself, your time, and your energy. If others are not saying thank you for all your hard work, then at the very least say it to yourself.

NOPE

As the nurturing, compassionate, giving females we are, it's often hard for us to say no to others. We want to help everyone — all the time! But when our family, friends, and colleagues ask for favors, and we oblige without a second thought, we're taking precious time and resources away from our self-care. That doesn't mean we should never agree to help others. Of course we should! All it means is that we need to choose our "yeses" more carefully.

"But Sheira," you say, *"I don't want to offend anyone who needs my help! If I say no, I'll come across like a selfish jerk."*

Not true. There are diplomatic and compassionate ways to say anything. And, for those who refuse to understand, you might want to take a look at the relationship and see whether it's based on mutual respect. As they say, "If everyone likes you, you're trying too hard!"

Girls, let's say you're feeling overwhelmed with too many obligations, when your friend Ashley says, "Can you help me with this English project tonight? You were super helpful last time." You can say yes immediately, *or* you can say, "I'm glad I was able to help out last time, but I'm actually feeling pretty overwhelmed right now with my own projects. I'm sorry, Ash. Check with me again if you need help next time and hopefully I'll be able to do it."

Let's say your daughter forgot she had to bring in an item for school, remembers only the night before, and has a really strict teacher. You can say, "I understand that you forgot. If I had advanced notice, I would have certainly picked it up for you when I was out. Next time, make sure to give me more of a heads-up. You'll need to take responsibility and tell your teacher you forgot. Either she'll understand or you'll have to take the hit on your grade."

Start to value yourself and, trust me, others will follow suit.

THE GOOD, THE BAD, AND THE UGLY

When I get up in the morning, before my feet even touch the floor, I think of five things I'm grateful for. I simply visualize them in my mind. Some people prefer to document these in a gratitude journal. Some enter it into their cell phone reminders where they can see it every day. Use whatever method works for you to awaken a genuine sense of gratitude every day. The big-ticket items I generally take the time to acknowledge are: (1) my health and the health of my family, (2) my functioning senses (how easily we take for granted our ability to taste things, hold a hand, hear a bird sing, watch a setting sun, or inhale a glorious scent!), (3) the clothes on my back, (4) the food on my plate, and (5) my dog. I have to say, my dog has taught me more valuable lessons about how to live life than pretty much any person I've ever met. Not looking to diss humans, but if you have a dog... right?

Sometimes, I find it helpful to focus on the small-ticket items as well — things like hugging my son (and that he still lets me), or watching my favorite movie, or making someone laugh with one of my corny jokes! I especially enjoy doing small but meaningful pay-it-forward acts with people in service positions because I believe they get a raw deal. I'll put a large tip in the tip jar at a coffee shop, help the supermarket check-out clerk bag my groceries, or give a warm smile and say "Hey, how's it going?" to the drive-thru attendant. These people are serving us day in and day out, and some of them are treated as though they are invisible. You can tell so much about a person from the way they treat those who serve.

Take an extra few seconds to put a smile on the
face of someone who serves you whether it be
the drive-thru attendant, the post office clerk,
or the waiter refilling your water glass.

Other times, I focus on the challenging things for which I'm grateful. I started this chapter off with the example of turning my resentment for my mother into an exercise of gratitude. Sometimes we can't see the lesson in the horrible things we're going through until some time has passed. However, if we're aware that whatever difficult situation we're experiencing right now will eventually teach us something, then we can, right now, be grateful for its occurrence. Cultivating gratitude for all of it — the good, the bad, and the downright hideous — is a skill that, when practiced on a daily basis, can help shift the way we look at life.

LITTLE MIRACLES

When I gave birth, I literally lost my mind. I remember being so over-whelmed (in the best possible way) at seeing this tiny person come out of me. And when they said, "It's a girl!," forget it. I remember repeating "Oh my G-d" over and over until I couldn't see straight. The doctor and my husband looked at each other wondering, "Is she okay?"

Once I brought this little miracle home, I found myself staring at her non-stop, noticing every little movement, facial expression, gaze, and coo. I was completely and utterly smitten. I cried every half hour for about three months. It didn't even matter that she looked exactly like my husband (I'm not kidding, it was like someone 'Shrinky-Dinked' his head and placed it in on her newborn body.)

Fast forward a few years. Seemingly overnight our daughters grow up. As they do, some of us may lose a bit of that sense of awe, wonder, and gratitude for their very being. Sometimes those emotions even get replaced with negative ones, such as irritation, impatience, and judgment. For some, it stems from the fact that we have deeply held beliefs that our daughters are a reflection of us. That's a lot of pressure to put on them. Our daughters are not our "mini-me's" or "show dogs" to parade around. They are their own people with their own opinions, desires, and souls. And, isn't that what we want for them? To be independent and create the lives that will make them the happiest? We need to allow them to become themselves — not who we think they should be (or even worse, who we wish we could have been).

Tip of the day: the next time your daughter walks into the room, take a minute to look at her. I mean deeply look at her with that sense of awe, wonder, and gratitude that you experienced when they first handed her to you, all wrapped up in that little receiving blanket. Look at her as the separate human being she is and allow *her* essence, *her* passion, and *her* personality to shine through.

Regularly telling her what a gift she is in your life sets the stage for a bond that can only strengthen over time. Your daughter needs to know and hear that you are grateful for her even when she's losing it, having a bad day, or copping some major attitude. You may not always approve of her behavior, but you must always be thankful that she is and always will be your little girl.

No matter what age your daughter is, never lose that sense of wonder at the miracle she is in your life.

A POEM FOR YOU!

I wrote this poem during a difficult and disconnected time in my life. After finishing it, I felt a true sense of appreciation to the universe for offering me the right words to express exactly what I was missing, which was a connection to myself.

When our energy is fried
From being preoccupied
We might be missing out
On what it's all about

A word, a glance, a touch
Can mean so very much
It's how we stay connected
In a world that's so infected

A world that's so damn busy
It can sometimes make you dizzy
And might not let you see
Your true priorities

So let's take a look around
And from time to time rebound
And truly be together
Cause we do not have forever

Time does not stand still
It flies by against our will
So let us take a minute
And simply just be in it

That way when we look back
We will not see a lack
But rather be elated
At the joy that we created

Key THANKFULNESS Takeaways:

- Write down 5 things for which you're thankful (preferably not material things) and put the list where you'll see it every day (bathroom mirror, cell phone, bedroom ceiling). You can't be grateful and bitter at the same time, so which do you choose?

- Show gratitude when people aren't necessarily expecting it. Thank your parents for the little things they do. Moms, say thank you to your daughters simply for being your daughters.

- Remember "Have-ta" vs "Want-ta" — it will help keep things in perspective

EXPRESSION

Watch my passion grow

T here's no one else on planet Earth exactly like you, not one other humanoid. Nobody has the same fingerprint, voiceprint, or taste buds as you. Nobody has the exact same upbringing, talents, or personality quirks as you. You are the only one of you there is!

In theory, knowing that you are truly one-of-a-kind should make you proud — but for many girls and women, it's not a source of pride at all. We live in a society where standing out can cause embarrassment, and fitting in is something to aspire to. But why? If you saw an interesting shirt, poster, or book, only to find out that there was only one of them in the whole world... wouldn't you think it was special? Wouldn't you want to keep it? Of course you would! You'd feel super cool! So why would you treat your wonderfully unique self any differently?

You're here for a reason. And that reason is, in short, to BE YOU! You contribute so much simply by being your authentic self. It's time to not only be who you are in private, but grace the world with all that you (and only you) have to offer. Express *yourself*!

Expression is the process of making your thoughts and feelings known. It's how we convey who we are as individuals. Expression can take many forms: the things we say, ways we behave, hobbies we practice, clothes we wear, careers we choose, and so on. And just like us, our expressions are 100% original. No two expressions are exactly alike. Even those of twins! I can say this for certain because, as you saw in the Halftime Show, I am one.

What you probably don't know is that we are identical! I know what you're thinking: "Holy cow, there are two of you lunatics?" Indeed, I'm afraid there are. We look alike, sound alike… but we are not totally alike. First of all, I smell better. Second of all, we are mirror twins, so many of the physical things I do in one direction (cross my arms, do a cartwheel, hold a deck of cards) she does in the opposite direction. Third of all, we have grown to be mirror twins in some personality-based ways as well. She's organized, I'm spontaneous. She's science-based, I'm faith-based. She a bit anxious, I'm the "happy idiot." Of course, there's a nurture-induced component to our differences, but the fact remains that we share genetic code and are still opposites in some very fundamental ways.

Even two peas in a pod
aren't exactly the same.

Twin or no twin, it's important to own your individuality. Take the time to figure out what makes you *you*. Pay attention to your prefer-ences, tendencies, interests, and aspirations — even if you think they're "weird" or "out there" — because one day you're going to need them.

IT'S ALIVE!

What do you want to be when you grow up? When we ask this ques-tion to young children, their eyes light up.

"A policeman!"

"A ballerina!"

"An astronaut!"

"A teacher!"

They see themselves in that role with full conviction and no hesitation! They believe!

Kids have an incredible ability to envision things clearly in their mind's eye, even though they may lack the consciousness and understanding of what it will take to get there. They *are* what they believe they are. I have to admit that I sometimes envy their cluelessness. No one has yet tried to squash their dreams by saying something like, "You don't *really* want to be a doctor, do you? Schooling takes years and you have to be on call all the time!" or "Don't be an actor. You won't be able to support yourself!" or "Not many girls are policemen, honey… that's a cute idea, though!" Kids are pure and untainted by fear, doubt, insecurity, and skepticism. Imagine what we could accomplish if we were that way.

So… what do *you* love to do? What makes time flow so effortlessly that three hours feels like ten minutes? What gets you excited? What makes you feel *alive*? Whether it's writing, drawing, playing an instrument, planning your friend's birthday party, rearranging your closet, collecting exotic bugs, building robots, or anything else — you must identify it. If you let your dreams go unattended for too long, the avalanche of life known as "the real world" can take over. The way to avoid that is to get in touch with your inner voice… and let it out!

Do what makes you feel alive, and
don't give a hootenanny what
anyone else thinks about it.

SEEN BUT NOT HEARD

Young girls have unlimited vision and imagination. They interact, communicate, and play with eagerness, energy, and enthusiasm! When they begin to approach adolescence, however, their self-esteem starts to plummet. Researchers call it "loss of voice" or "the confidence gap," and it's happening much earlier and more intensely than it did in previous generations.

Psychologist Roni Cohen-Sandler, author of *Easing Their Stress: Helping Them Thrive in the Age of Pressure*, cites increased stress levels and more frequent psychological crises as the main explanation for "the confidence gap." In her words, "They are so busy living up to others' expectations that they either don't develop or eventually relinquish their own goals. They are so focused on achieving external emblems of success that they don't get the chance to figure out what really excites them and gives them pleasure. They barely know who they are or who they want to be."

Another explanation for "the confidence gap" unfortunately comes from each of us. In her insightful book *Untangled: Guiding Teenage Girls Through The Seven Transitions Into Adulthood*, Lisa Damour, PhD reveals: "Girls, more than boys, may be derailed by disappointment because research shows that they explain failure differently than boys do. When a boy fails a test, doesn't get the lead in a play or faces some other hitch in his plans, he's likely to attribute his difficulties to external or temporary factors. He'll say, "It was a dumb test," "The drama teacher doesn't like me," or "I didn't even want to do that anyway." Right or wrong, a boy's explanation can help him to feel that he's still in the running. Girls, on the other hand, are more likely to explain failures in terms of internal, permanent factors: she's broken and can't be fixed. When faced with disappointment, a girl might say, "I'm no good at this," despite piles of contradictory evidence. Worst of all, girls' explanations for failure take them out of the game. Once a girl decides that she's weak in something, it doesn't matter if she's smart or talented; she's likely to stop trying to build her skills and thus surrenders her chance at success."

Why is it so easy for females to give encouragement to friends and family, but not offer that same beautiful gesture to ourselves?

By internalizing this dynamic, we can start to see why we give up on ourselves so easily. Think of all the smart, strong, skilled girls and women in your life and in the world. Where would they be if they had given up on themselves after being defeated, making mistakes, or getting off track? Nowhere, that's where! And the irony of it all is that most girls and women tell their friends and peers to "Keep going," "Hang in there," and "Go for it!" Why don't we give ourselves the same pep talk? We need to replace the negative connotations in our dialogue with positive ones; it's known as a "growth mindset." Research shows that girls with growth mindsets outperform those with fixed mindsets. Instead of asking "Why *can't* I do this?," ask, "How *can* I do this?" Open up your mind and give yourself another chance instead of giving up. When you persevere, you're being kind to yourself (and you know how I feel about that). We're stronger than we think, ladies, and it's high time we realized that.

FULL S.T.E.A.M. AHEAD

STEM is an acronym referring to the academic disciplines of Science, Technology, Engineering, and Mathematics (some educators expanded the acronym to STEAM which includes an 'A' for "Arts" to emphasize the importance of this field in innovation. I couldn't agree more!). In the past decade or so, it has become a staple of educational discourse and an acknowledgment of the inadequate curricula (and resulting shortage of skilled workers) in these areas. As Wikipedia explains, "Maintaining a citizenry that is well versed in the STEM fields is a key portion of the public education agenda of the United States."

Sadly but truly, the national focus on STEM has more to do with the United States maintaining its competitive edge in the global market-place than encouraging a love of learning in these fields. Having said that, just because our country's interests can often be narrow-minded doesn't mean yours should be too. Girls who are attracted to these fields should fully and wholeheartedly pursue them. Many teen girls, over a long period of time, have rejected these interests, not wanting to come across as "nerds" or "geeks" by showing interest in things like physics, statistics, computer science, robotics, engineering, nanotechnology, etc. All of these industries could potentially bring girls great fulfillment, joy, and success — but instead of being true to who they are, some girls choose the "safe route," for fear of being judged or targeted by their peers.

My message to those girls? STOP THAT AT ONCE! Guess what? Middle school and high school last seven short years. Are you going to let the opinions of a bunch of teenagers determine your happiness for the next 80-100 years? I can relate to the suggested importance of being accepted by those around you. The things your peers find cool now are not necessarily the things they will find cool a few short years from now. I promise you, if you go to your 10-year high school reunion as the head of Nanotechnology for Google, everyone will think you are very, very cool. Also, guess what? Cool means different things to different people. If you have a passion for medicine and you want to do research, that's pretty freakin' cool. In the future, you'll prefer being uncool in the eyes of a random former classmate than regretful for not pursuing the one thing you really wanted to do.

Thankfully, the world is opening up, boundaries are expanding, and there is more encouragement than ever for girls to enter these traditionally male-dominated careers. Companies like Goldie Blox and organizations like Girls Who Code have made it their mission to inspire the next generation of female innovators. If this is something that speaks to you, see Resources in the back for more STEM-related opportunities.

FOREVER JUNG

Psychiatrist and psychotherapist Carl Jung once said, "The greatest unconscious force in the lives of children is the unfulfilled dreams of their parents." And thus, we find another culprit on the long road to Insecurityville: the pressure put on young girls by their sometimes overbearing (but generally well-intentioned) moms. As much as we hate to admit it, many moms unwittingly impose the anguish of our own abandoned ambitions onto our daughters. For example, the mom who wants her daughter to be a lawyer after she herself went to law school and had to drop out; the mom who dissuades her daughter from auditioning for musical theater because she herself couldn't hack it in the competitive, predatory world of show biz; the mom who pressures her daughter to take over the family business because she herself was the one who created it, and wants it to live on.

By forcing these inappropriate expectations on our daughters, we're literally sucking the life out of them. We can do our daughters no greater favor in life than allowing them to fully express who *they* are without judgment, in ways both obvious and subtle. Sure, maybe she pirouetted in the living room at age three, or used a brush as a microphone at age eight. But maybe she also took the pots and pans out of the cabinet and banged on them endlessly with wooden spoons. Maybe she jumped in muddy puddles and played with earthworms and spiders. If you told her repeatedly (and angrily) to stop, you were — perhaps unbeknownst to yourself — squelching her unique form of expression. We need to let our girls explore! If we allow them to trust their intuition about what makes them happy from a young age, they will become more likely to trust their intuition in other parts of their lives as they get older.

So the question becomes: moms, how are you treating yourselves when it comes to your own unique form of expression? Are you fulfilled with your work (whether it's inside or outside the home)? Are you putting your talents and gifts to good use? Are you doing what brings you joy? If the answer to any or all of those questions is "not really," then make a change. Plant that garden you've always wanted in the backyard. Finally learn how to play the violin. Leave your miserable old job and find a new one. It doesn't matter how big or small your desire is. Does it make your aorta pump hemoglobin into your ventricles at twice its normal rate? Does it make the hair on your arms stand up when you think about it? Does it make your lips turn slowly upward into a permanent smile on your happy little face? Then do it.

If you're not exactly sure what it is that floats your boat, that's okay! Everyone's journeying on their own path, uncovering things at their own pace, and discovering themselves in their own time. Don't force it. Just be open. A potential clue might lie in thinking back on places, people, and activities you enjoyed earlier in life. Our childhood memories in particular can be super powerful. The more we connect to them, the more we connect to ourselves.

May your heart sing, may your soul fly,
may your goals and daydreams never die.

GIRL POWAAAHH!!

This whole gender equality movement is a real thing and it's entering the transition phase. For those who don't know the clinical terminology, there are three phases of labor: the early stage, active stage, and finally, transition stage. The early stage of the fight for gender equality began in the 1920s when women petitioned for and finally received the right to vote. The active stage was the 1960s and 1970s when women were encouraged to break out of their singular mother/wife roles and enter the workforce. The old-fashioned idea of the "housewife" was slowly but surely being dismantled. The transition phase is often most intense phase, and also the one with the shortest duration. That's the phase we're in now. In the last few years, the issue of equal pay for equal work has risen to the forefront of the political landscape. Legislation against sexual harassment has also increased, and is getting closer to the gaining its rightful amount of attention in the public eye. Campaigns like Dove's "Real Beauty," Always' "Like A Girl," Nike's "Girl Effect," Lean In's "Ban Bossy," and many other female-focused initiatives are taking center stage on the internet, and exploding on social media. When corporations and organizations make that kind of investment (in terms of both time and money), it means that our society is beginning to validate the need for there to be more "girl in our world"! Our rallying cry over the last 100 years to have our contributions, gifts, and voices be valued is finally being heard. But the fight is far from over.

If you ever felt like you wanted to do something, but were scared of failing, being judged, or falling short, consider this: don't do it for yourself. Do it for women everywhere. We have come way too far to turn back now. If women stop chasing their dreams, the fight for gender equality may as well be over. This country was built on the audacious, outrageous dreams of females like you and me. And anyone who ever did anything worthwhile, started out not knowing what the *heck* they were doing.

No ballerina started off as a prima, no doctor operated on her first day on the job, no model didn't fall on her butt at least once going down the catwalk, and no public speaker's first speech was flawlessly delivered. But by continuing to go after what they wanted and *succeeding*, they contributed greatly to this century-old fight for overdue liberties. You need to do the same.

FOLLOW YOUR BLISS

My generation wasn't specifically taught to "pursue our passion" or "follow our bliss," but my two personal boat-floaters have always been children and music. Ever since I was little, I was one of those girls who was naturally drawn to young kids. I wanted to hug them, talk to them, play with them, and nurture them… sometimes to my own detriment. Flashback: When I was six years old, my parents took us to a family sleep away camp in upstate New York (in case you were wondering, yes, that is weird). Living in the bunk next door was a family with the most adorable two-year old son. His mother said I was too young to hold him, but when all the kids were playing in the yard one afternoon, I snuck over to pick him up, and promptly dropped him on his head. Thanks to the soft spot on his cranium, he didn't get hurt… but boy, did I get in trouble!

My love of music was also instilled in me from a young age. When I was eight years old, my mother taught me how to play guitar. When I turned 11, after having begged my parents for years, I began classical piano lessons. So of course, six months later when I told my parents I was quitting (practicing was such a drag) they wouldn't hear of it. Over the years, I probably said I was quitting about 60 times, but I never did. Eventually, I did give up Chopin, Beethoven, and Mozart, but only to start composing my own melodies! Over time, those little ditties turned into full songs. And little did I know that one day I would combine my two passions into an actual career!

It didn't start out that way, though. My journey was, and continues to be, a long and winding road.

When I graduated college, I took a crappy-paying job at a top advertising firm in New York City because I wanted to get into writing jingles. (This, after graduating Magna Cum Laude from Business School. Needless to say, my parents were thrilled). While working, I was writing and recording my own songs on the side. After a year and a half I was laid off from the firm when it lost its largest client, Burger King. I then got a job at an entertainment law firm with high marquis clients like Billy Joel, Whitney Houston, Madonna, and Bruce Springsteen. My hope was to use that position as a steppingstone to a record industry gig. I was still *writing and recording my songs on the side.* My boss at the law firm made a deal with me that I would work as his assistant for a year, and then he would help me get a job in the music biz. I kept my commitment and he kept his promise. I was 24 years old when I landed a job with a very cool start-up record label as the assistant to the VP of Marketing, and worked my way up to Director of Advertising over the course of my seven years there. And the whole time, I was still *writing and recording my songs on the side.*

Four and a half years into my record company job, I gave birth to my first child. At that time, I was taking a songwriting workshop in Manhattan and the consistent feedback was that my style was catchy, melodic, and theatrical. When I shared that with my husband — being the super creative and intuitive media professional that he is — he suggested that I write a children's song about a teddy bear since he knew how much I love kids. Ten minutes later, I had a full song (music and lyrics) called "My Teddy Bear." The next day, I wrote another kids' song, and another the following day. A few weeks later, when I had about 10 songs written, my husband pursued a connection he had at our local public television station and presented some of my songs to them.

They said the timing was impeccable since they were looking to co-produce an original children's show. And voila, "Dittydoodle Works" was born! I had found my true musical calling by combining my passions.

Love of kids + love of music = writing children's songs!

Alongside my corporate career over the next 10 years (yes, 10!), we nurtured this children's property through producing short music videos, store appearances, and eventually selling out mall tours. At this point, I was working in marketing for a technology company. As fate would have it, while "Dittydoodle Works" was gaining traction, the company was going through some serious turmoil and there were rumblings of layoffs. Day by day, HR was calling people in to notify them of their fate. Then my day came. I returned home later that afternoon, greeted my family with a very sad face, and then promptly broke out into a ho-down in the living room, chanting "Mommy got laid off! Mommy got laid off!" (to the tune to of "Nanny Nanny Poo Poo"). That very same day, my husband closed on the funding to produce 26 half-hour episodes of "Dittydoodle Works." The stars had finally aligned! And it only took 18 years!

Over the next four years, I had my dream job of writing songs and being the singing voice for one of the main characters! We moved the company from our home office into an 18,000 square foot facility where we produced, shot, and edited 40 episodes of the show. I wrote over 180 songs, recorded with one of Broadway's top music producers, and collaborated with some legendary talent. Words cannot describe the elation and gratitude I felt at having been given this incredible opportunity — bringing joy to children through my music.

THE RUG PULLED OUT FROM UNDER ME

There's a song called "Anyway" written by Martina McBride, Brett Warren, and Brad Warren (have to give props to the songwriters).

The song talks about the power of creativity, perseverance, and faith even in the face of adversity:

> *You can spend your whole life building something from nothin'*
> *One storm can come and blow it all away*
> *Build it anyway*
>
> *You can chase a dream that seems so out of reach*
> *And you know it might not ever come your way*
> *Dream it anyway*

After finally having the opportunity to bring the show nationwide, the economy collapsed in 2008 and the show lost its funding. Our hopes and dreams to mass market the property and get it into retail were dashed.

In May 2009, we had to close the doors to our beautiful studio and lay everyone off. It was one of the hardest periods of my life. Beyond the devastating disappointment of losing my dream job, my husband and I still had to provide for our children (who were then 11 and 15). We felt lost and directionless. Given that we both came from marketing backgrounds, my husband was able to secure a couple of clients and I helped him while also doing some freelance assignments. We barely scraped by. It was a dark period for both of us. At times, we turned against each other not understanding how our beautiful dream could crash and burn so quickly just as we were on the edge of it taking flight.

In the years since, alongside yet another corporate job, I've had bursts of creativity mixed with periods of feeling deeply sorry for myself. I tried to stay true to my passions by writing for Songs of Love, an amazing organization that gifts personalized songs to sick children around the country. I also developed the "Motiv8" empowerment program for mothers and daughters which I present at a variety of different venues all across the country. Doing the program led me to writing a book (yes, the one you're reading)... and who knows what will come next!

The road to pursuing your passion is never a straight line. It's winding, curvy, and unpredictable. Perseverance, determination, and belief in your passion are some of the keys to staying the course — but when life gets in the way (and get in the way it will), you need to remember to go with the flow and just glide. As much as you may want to, don't fight it. Just understand that the universe has pressed the "pause" button for a reason. I've experienced many highs and lows in my life: careers given, careers taken away; people given, people taken away; chances given, chances taken away. It happens to everyone, every day, all around the world. Don't take it personally. If you find yourself in a similar situation of dead ends and detours, just keep going. The tides will turn. Society needs your strong voice, your unbridled talent, and your creativity to help create a world that's more innovative, intuitive, and balanced.

To give up on yourself is to give up on the world. When you close yourself to your true gift, you deny it to someone out there who might truly need it.

EXPRESS YOURSELF

The first step to pursuing your passion (big or small) is surrounding yourself with like-minded, supportive, and equally passionate people. Most people think linearly and can't understand the dreamer's vision, and it's very easy to get sucked into others' opinions of why you *shouldn't* do something. They'll give you a million reasons why implementing it is impossible or unrealistic. Some people have the genuine intention of saving you from pain or disappointment, and others simply don't want you to be more successful than they are. Remember: take it from whom it comes.

Mark Twain said, "Stay away from people who belittle your ambitions. Small people always do that, but the really great make you feel like you, too, can become great!"

Girls and moms: If you want to move a passion or career forward, start by joining a relevant club in school, enrolling in an afterschool program, doing volunteer work, starting a meetup, going to networking events — do whatever you have to do to expand your circles, grow your knowledge base, and be with people who "get you."

Another critical step is to find a mentor: someone who has been where you are, and can provide you with advice, encouragement, and pearls of wisdom. Don't be intimidated by someone who has more experience or success than you. We're all human. Everybody poops. Remember that.

Let's say your passion is food, but your school doesn't offer cooking classes and community programs are too expensive. Why not call your favorite local restaurant and see if the head chef there would be willing to talk to you? I'm a huge believer in "if you don't ask, you don't get," and amazing things have happened to me when I simply *went for it*. The worst that could happen is that they say "No." If you want to be successful in life, you better get used to that word, and then keep going until you get a "Yes"!

You only go around once in this lifetime.
Take risks and go for it. The universe is
rooting for you!

Lastly, if your passion seems too overwhelming as a whole, simply break it down into smaller, bite-size pieces. Let's say you want start an online business selling jewelry that you created. Start off by breaking it down into several smaller steps:

1. Research different jewelry sites for creative ideas.
2. Investigate raw materials needed.
3. Call a local jewelry store and talk to the owner about how they got their start.
4. Check out a YouTube video tutorial on building a simple e-commerce website.

Keep listing the steps until you have a comprehensive checklist. Then, attach a realistic timeline to each step, and find a friend to keep you accountable (especially if you struggle with discipline issues).

THE LAW OF ATTRACTION

The Law of Attraction has received much attention (and an equal amount of controversy) over the years. The premise of the law, captured in the movie and book of the same name, is that we attract what we think about most. But I came across this phrase that resonated with me more:

"We don't attract what we want. We attract what we believe."

If you believe you have what it takes and act on it, you will attract opportunities, situations, and people who align with that belief. If, on the other hand, you believe that you're not good enough, smart enough, or capable enough, you will continue to attract opportunities, situations, and people that prove that to be true (mostly in the form of procrasti-nation and resistance).

Decide which category you fall under. You may say you believe you're capable, but if deep down you're feeding yourself lies that you're not, then you need to get real. Always listen to the underlying thoughts (the thoughts *behind* the thoughts aka your subconscious); they tell the true story of what's going on for you.

There are many ways to reprogram your mind into believing what you want to believe. The key is to offer yourself more helpful thoughts and to do so consistently. A great book on this topic is Shad Helmstetter's *What To Say When You Talk To Yourself.* The author compares our brains to computers: like a computer's software program, which acts upon its instructions, so too do our brains act on the codes of our subconscious thoughts. The most powerful words are the ones we say to ourselves. Please choose them wisely.

PASS IT ON

When I was pregnant for the first time, I didn't know if I was having a boy or girl. I was taking a songwriting workshop in New York City at the time, and one of the assignments was to write a song for the holi-days. The following are the lyrics to that song. When I read them now, it amazes me… because I feel like I predicted the future! Turns out I did have a daughter, and I did, in fact, pass on the gift of song. She is a breathtaking singer-songwriter in her own right and I'm so honored to have her amazing talent featured on two of the songs for this book project. I guess it was "beshert" (Hebrew for "meant to be")!

The Gift Of Song
© Sheira Brayer

"The Gift of Song" is available on most digital platforms including iTunes and Spotify.

Here is my present to you sweet child
It can make you sad it can make you smile
It's not a doll or a game or toy
But it will bring you eternal joy

Chorus:

The gift of song
Will keep you young forever
Will bring your friends and family together
You can't outgrow or lose
The gift of song

Music always seems to be
The one thing that breeds harmony
I hope one day my little girl
You'll use your voice to heal the world

CHORUS

You must always strive
To keep this precious gift alive
Remember to pass it on
To the next generation

CHORUS

CHILDREN ARE OUR GREATEST TEACHERS

Life is a journey, and a short one at that. We'd all do ourselves a big favor to take a lesson from our children when it comes to perseverance and belief. Have you ever seen a toddler learn to walk, fall a few times, and then just sit there saying, "You know what, Ma, this walking thing isn't really for me. Do me a fave' and pass me my bottle and those pureed bananas. I'm just gonna hang here."

Of course not! But this is what we do as we grow up! We give it a shot, but when it gets too hard, we immediately stop. Don't stop! You're worth more than that.

If you know what you're passionate about, make a commitment that you'll do whatever it takes to bring it to life. Do it full-time, part-time, or as a hobby — but just do it. It may be hard, and there may be obstacles and challenges along the way, but that shouldn't stop you. And if you already gave up on what makes your heart sing (no matter the reason) make a decision *today* — in fact *right now* — that you will get back on the horse that you abandoned and "build it anyway!"

Key EXPRESSION takeaways:

- Consider what makes you feel most alive while you're doing it. Take steps to follow that course. Even if it doesn't become your career, you can always make it a hobby. Remember, you never regret the things you do; only the things you don't do.

- Find someone you trust to be your mentor. They can guide and support you as you strive to reach your goals.

- Talk about your dreams and goals to others. Talking about it makes it more real. And making it real will attract the necessary resources and people.

- Write down your dreams and look at them regularly. Set goals and follow through on them. It's the hardest part but is the single most critical key to success!

BRINGING IT ON HOME

We all know the saying "treat others as you would want to be treated"… but have you ever heard the saying "treat yourself as you would want to be treated"? Probably not. I just made it up. But I made it up for a good reason! Despite what sappy romantic comedies will have you believe, you are the love of your own life. And if you don't make it a point to fall for yourself each and every day, you're missing out. I can talk for days on end about the importance of communication with others, respect for others, tolerance of others… but at the end of the day, it all starts with you.

Whether you're a mom, teenage girl, or somewhere in between, know this: your talents, quirks, insecurities, and imperfections are essential to this world. You're here for a reason, and it's up to you to decide what that is. Never let anyone tell you you're not good enough. Never let anyone tell you that you can't do something. Never let anyone tell you you're not deserving of all that the world has to offer. You are, and always will be.

If you take away one thing from this book and nothing else, let it be that you are your own life partner. I hope I've offered a glimpse of some of the skills that can help you be a partner you're proud to live with. Be kind. Be curious. Be daring. Be bold. Be you.

Now, go out there, you beautiful soul, and start rocking your own world!

ACKNOWLEDGEMENTS

There are so many people I need to thank for assisting me in giving birth to this creation (both written and musical). If I've inadvertently omitted anyone, I humbly ask for your forgiveness.

First and foremost, I want to thank my husband, Cory. If it weren't for your unwavering belief, enduring support, and occasional tough love nudge, this book would simply not be. Here's to another "Dreamseekers" success story. Thank you, Booba, for being on this crazy rollercoaster journey with me. What a ride, what a glorious ride!

Thank you also to my magnificent daughter, Ayden Skye, for your unparalleled contribution to the book and music. Your editorial insight, unique songwriting talent, and stunning voice literally made this project what it is. But beyond all that, it's the person that you are that I'm most proud of. I just love being with you. As I say in the song I wrote for you: "In my dreams there could never be a greater daughter than what you are to me. You give me love, laughter and inspiration; you give me hope for the next generation." I'll say it now and I'll say it for always — I'm the luckiest mama!

Thank you also to my incredible son, Liam. You unknowingly contributed to the book not just by being my son, but also by pursuing *your* passion with fierce determination. It's amazing when I think about the boy you were back then and the man you are today. Simply incredible! And let's not forget all the great books, quotes, and songs you've recommended, some of which directly influenced this project. You are a true inspiration to me and to everyone around you.

Spasiba Vam to my father. I wouldn't be half the person I am today if it weren't for you. The lessons you've taught me about tolerance, simplicity, humility, and the importance of family (even in the wake of yours being senselessly taken from you) will stay with me always. But the best part about being your daughter is having the ability to laugh and to see the bright side of life. You are a gem of a father and I love you with all my heart!

"Toda raba" to my mother. You are the reason I started on this path. It's been a journey of patience, forgiveness, and letting go. I so appreciate you giving me a name that means "song," as music has been and always will be my number one passion. I will continue to carry my name proudly and use it for good. Ani ohevet otach!

To my Loli Poli — thank you for your love and support as well as your insightful feedback. In many ways, we've been on this journey together. I consider us incredibly blessed — for being daughters to Mom, for the honor and privilege of being mothers to such incredible daughters, and most importantly, for the gift of your friendship, our insane sense of humor and our passion for music. Thank you for being my light.

Thank you also to my brother Ron: you've contributed to my life in ways you don't even know. You've taught me acceptance, presence, and simply letting things be. The lessons I've learned from being your sister are engrained in these pages, and for that I'm truly grateful.

To my dear friend Kenny: the time that you selflessly gave to review, format, and layout the book — I just don't have the words. You did an incredible job! I simply adore you and am so blessed to call you my best friend for the last &#@$* years. (Let's just say it's over 280 in dog years!)

Thank you Mary, for painstakingly, thoroughly, and thoughtfully offering your insights. You were my teacher in high school and, as it turns out, my teacher in life as well as my chosen sister! Could I be luckier? Methinks not.

Thank you to my mastermind group for your never-ending support and encouragement throughout this process — it has meant the world to me! And to those who participated in my virtual focus group: your input and feedback truly helped solidify the direction of the book and the music. Thank you from the bottom of my heart.

And lastly, my deep gratitude to those who've inspired my journey — whether through the written word in the hundreds of books I've devoured, videos I've watched, articles I've read, and songs I've been touched by. I plan on being forever a student until my last breath. The mere admission of "I don't know, but I want to learn" is what makes life's journey truly worthwhile.

RESOURCES

MUSIC THAT MOTIV8ES

Music has profoundly helped and continues to help me on my journey. Below is a list of songs related to each skill of Motiv8 (including my own songs). I hope they comfort you when you're down and inspire you when you're up!

Meditation

"Breathe" by Sheira Brayer (recorded with Andie Mechanic)
"The Sound of Silence" by Simon & Garfunkel
"Listen to the Rain" by Enya
"Slow Me Down" by Emmy Rossum
YouTube: The Most Relaxing Classical Music in the Universe
(Noah Johnson channel)

Optimism

"Change Your Mind" by Sheira Brayer
"Keep Your Head Up" by Andy Grammar
"Walking on Sunshine" by Katrina and the Waves
"Put Your Records On" by Corinne Bailey Rae
"Happy" by Pharrell

Tolerance

"We're All The Same" by Sheira Brayer (additional lyrics by Leora
"Loli" Brayer; sung by AnnMarie Milazzo)
"Ebony and Ivory" by Stevie Wonder
"Imagine" by John Lennon
"Peaceful World" by John Mellencamp

"What a Wonderful World" by Louis Armstrong
"Where is the Love" by The Black Eyed Peas

Intuition

"A Way Will Be Shown" by Sheira Brayer
"Scars To Your Beautiful" by Alessia Cara
"Intuition" by Jewel
"Listen to your Heart" by Roxette
"The Voice Within" by Christina Aguilera

Vibe

"Givin' It Out Again" by Leora "Loli" Brayer and Sheira Brayer
(sung by Tabitha Fair)
"Good Vibrations" by The Beach Boys
"Man in the Mirror" by Michael Jackson
"I Believe I Can Fly" by R. Kelly
"The Prayer" by Andrea Bocelli and Celine Dion

Attitude

"It's Not What You Say, It's How You Say It" by Sheira Brayer
 "More Than Words" by Extreme
"Teach Your Children" by Crosby, Stills and Nash
"You Gotta Be" by Des'ree
"The Living Years" by Mike and the Mechanics

Thankfulness

"Thank U" by Alanis Morissette (sung by Sheira Brayer and
Ayden Skye)
"Oh How the Years Go By" by Vanessa Williams
"Tomorrow" from the Annie soundtrack
"We Are Family" by Sister Sledge
"Bless the Broken Road" by Rascal Flatts

Expression

"Gift of Song" by Sheira Brayer
"Anyway" by Martina McBride
"Dream On" by Aerosmith
"I Hope You Dance" by Lee Ann Womack
"Girl on Fire" by Alicia Keys
"Express Yourself" by Madonna

MOVIES

These are films that made me scratch my head and say "Huh?", "Wow!", "OMG!", or "I never thought of it like that!":

"Embrace"
"Finding Kind"
"Race To Nowhere"
"I Am"
"The Boy in the Striped Pajamas"
"The Secret"
"Bully"
"What the Bleep Do We Know"

YOUTUBE VIDEOS

Videos that will make you re-think what you thought you knew and/or give you a renewed sense of perspective.

"Dad and daughter inspire with morning affirmations" (USA Today), Published Sept. 22, 2016

"The Scientific Power of Meditation (AsapSCIENCE), Published Jan. 18, 2015

"Katie Makkai Pretty (Clean)" (amanda2lloyd)

"What Your Daughter Hears When You Criticize Yourself" (Veriy), Published March 2, 2017

"Lily Myers Shrinking Women" (Button Poetry), Published April 18, 2013

"Your Body Language May Shape Who You Are / Amy Cuddy" (Ted Talk), Published Oct. 1, 2012

"Body Evolution — Model Before and After" (President of the World), Published May 22, 2012

"Look Up — Gary Turk Official Video" (Gary Turk), Published April 25, 2014

"How To Find a Mentor" (Mary Forleo), Published Sept. 13, 2016

"Do Schools Kill Creativity/Sir Ken Robinson" (Ted Talk), Published Jan. 6, 2007

"What If Millie Dresselhaus, Female Scientist, Was Treated Like a Celebrity" (General Electric), Published Feb. 8, 2017

QUOTES

I love quotes. They're an amazing way to distill and simplify a complicated concept or thought into a memorable bite size nugget. Let's start off with my favorite:

"Be the change you wish to see in the world." — Mahatma Gandhi

"Silence is true wisdom's best reply." — Euripides

"Whether you think you can or you can't; either way you are right." — Henry Ford

"Be sure to taste your words before you spit them out." — Unknown

"Stay away from people who belittle your ambitions. Small people always do that, but the really great make you feel like you, too, can become great!" — Mark Twain

"The richest person is not the one who has the most, but the one who needs the least." — Unknown

"The greatest unconscious force in the lives of children is the unfulfilled dreams of their parents." — Carl Jung

"There is nothing permanent except change" — Heraclitus

"Life isn't about waiting for the storms to pass; it's about learning to dance in the rain." — Vivian Greene

"No one can make you feel inferior without your consent."
— Eleanor Roosevelt

"Be yourself. Everyone else is already taken." — Oscar Wilde

BOOKS

These and many other books have had a profound impact on me and the way I perceive myself and the world around me. Each one is a gem.

Daring Greatly by Brené Brown, PhD
The Five Love Languages (For Parents/For Teens) by Gary Chapman
What To Say When You Talk To Yourself by Shad Helmstetter
Man's Search For Meaning by Victor Frankl
Mothering and Daughtering by Sil and Eliza Reynolds
Loving What Is by Byron Katie
You Are A Badass by Jen Sincero
The Power of Now by Eckhardt Tolle
Codependent No More by Melody Beattie
You'll See It When You Believe It by Dr. Wayne Dyer
Blessing of a Skinned Knee by Wendy Mogel, PhD
The Charge by Brendon Burchard
The Four Agreements by Don Miguel Ruiz
The War of Art by Steven Pressfield

WEBSITES

A few websites to help you get started with some of the tools in the book.

Transcendental Meditation: **http:www.tm.org**.
Introduction to Non-violent Communication: **www.cnvc.org**
The Work by Byron Katie: **http://thework.com/en**
The Collaborative for Academic, Social, and Emotional Learning
(CASEL): **http://www.casel.org**
Edutopia (Social Emotional Learning): **edutopia.org**
Department of Education (STEM): **www.ed.gov/stem**

MISCELLANEOUS

Just some extra stuff you might like:

"Comes The Dawn" — poem by Veronica Shoffstall
Headspace (meditation app)
TUT "Notes From The Universe"
"Love Is…" — essay by Michael Crichton (yes, the Jurassic Park dude)
"Teaching Peace In Elementary Schools" — article by Julie Scelfo
(New York Times, November 14, 2015)

NOTES

Page 2 – *Mean Girls*, motion picture directed by Mark Waters, written by Rosalind Wiseman (book), Tina Fey (screenplay), Paramount Pictures, M.G. Films, Broadway Video, 2004

Page 2 – *Finding Kind*, movie (documentary), directed by Lauren Parsekian, Shady Acres Entertainment, Distributed by IndieFlix, 2011

Page 7 – Motivation is never the first step in making things happen. John Maxwell *Failing Forward: Turning Mistakes into Stepping Stones for Success*, Harper Collins, Nashville, TN, 2007

Page 8 – Dr. Wayne Dyer, *You'll See It When You Believe It*, Quill an Imprint of Harper Collins Publishers, New York 1989

Page 13 – If you don't go within, you'll go without. Quote by Viktor E. Frankl, author of *A Man's Search For Meaning*

Page 17 – Bruce Almighty, motion picture directed by Tom Shadyac, written by Steve Koren, Mark O'Keefe and Steve Oedekerk, Universal Pictures, USA, 2003

Page 81 – Esther and Jerry Hicks, *Ask and It Is Given: Learning to Manifest the Law of Attraction*, Hay House, United States, 2004

Page 82 – Masuro Emoto, *The Hidden Message of Water*, Translated by David Thayne, Beyond Words Publishing, Inc., 2005

Page 84 – Amy Cuddy *"Your body language shapes who you are"* video on TedGlobal 2012

Page 92 – Learn more about Non-Violent Communication at **www.cnvc.org**

Page. 98 – Stephen Covey, *The 7 Habits of Highly Effective People*, The Free Press, United States, 1989

Page 104 – Byron Katie *Loving What Is: Four Questions That Can Change Your Life*, Harmony Books, New York, 2003

Page 106 – "Resentment is like drinking poison expecting the other person to die." Quote by Malachy McCourt.

Page 108 – I Am, motion picture written and directed by Tom Shadyac, Flying Eye Productions, USA 2010

Page 126 – Roni Cohen-Sandler, PhD, *Easing Their Stress: Helping Our Girls Thrive in the Age of Pressure*, Author & Company, New York, 2012

Page 126 – Lisa Damour, PhD, *"Untangled: Guiding Teenage Girls Through the Seven Transitions Into Adulthood"*, Ballantine Books, New York 2016

Page 129 – Learn more about Girls Who Code at https://girlswhocode.com/ and Goldieblox at http://www.goldieblox.com/

Page 134 – Martina McBride *"Anyway"*, composed by Brett Warren, Brad Warren and Martina McBride, RCA Records, Released 2007

ABOUT THE AUTHOR

Sheira Brayer is a New York-based motivational speaker and multiple award-winning songwriter. She spent over a decade as the co-creator and head songwriter of "Dittydoodle Works," the Emmy-nominated and nationally distributed children's television series, for which she wrote more than 200 songs. Sheira has also used songwriting to contribute charitably, composing custom songs for sick children through the Songs of Love Foundation, as well as the theme song for the esteemed Wounded Warrior Project[®].

In 2012, Sheira created Motiv8: 8 Ways To ROCK Your Own World, an interactive female empowerment program for women and girls. The multimedia experience melds together music, humor, personal anecdotes, and proven communication methods to teach audiences how to be the best version of themselves they can be. Sheira continues to present Motiv8 all across the country to rave reviews.

In addition to being a tenacious creative force, Sheira is also a mother of two, a wife of one, and a friend of basically everyone she encounters. She lives with her husband in Dix Hills, NY.

More at www.sheirabrayer.com.